P9-CCM-976

IT'S NOT SO HARD TO SPEND A TRILLION OR SO A YEAR—IF YOU KNOW HOW

You can build a huge hospital and forget
to equip it with telephones.

You can continue to stockpile helium
for a blimp air force.

You can conduct a massive research project into
how long it takes to change a lightbulb.

You can deliberately sink your own ships
with immense amounts of valuable
equipment aboard.

You can buy back missiles you gave
away for free to allies who have turned into
international outlaws.

You can hire efficiency experts who cost more
money than they can cut.

STUPID GOVERNMENT TRICKS

JOHN J. KOHUT is a political analyst who has been
collecting strange news clippings for over a decade, and
is the coauthor of the News of the Weird book series and
News from the Fringe. He lives in Washington, D.C.

STUPID GOVERNMENT TRICKS

Outrageous (but True!) Stories of Bureaucratic Bungling and Washington Waste

---

John J. Kohut

Illustrated by Drew Friedman

A PLUME BOOK

PLUME
Published by the Penguin Group
Penguin Books USA Inc., 375 Hudson Street,
New York, New York 10014, U.S.A.
Penguin Books Ltd, 27 Wrights Lane,
London W8 5TZ, England
Penguin Books Australia Ltd, Ringwood,
Victoria, Australia
Penguin Books Canada Ltd, 10 Alcorn Avenue,
Toronto, Ontario, Canada M4V 3B2
Penguin Books (N.Z.) Ltd, 182–190 Wairau Road,
Auckland 10, New Zealand

Penguin Books Ltd, Registered Offices:
Harmondsworth, Middlesex, England

First published by Plume, an imprint of Dutton Signet,
a division of Penguin Books USA Inc.

First Printing, April, 1995
10 9 8 7 6 5 4 3 2 1

Copyright © John J. Kohut, 1995
Illustrations copyright © Drew Friedman, 1995
All rights reserved
Portions of this book appeared in *Playboy* and the *San Jose Mercury News*.

 REGISTERED TRADEMARK—MARCA REGISTRADA

LIBRARY OF CONGRESS CATALOGING-IN-PUBLICATION DATA:

Kohut, John J.
  Stupid government tricks : outrageous (but true!) stories of bureaucratic bungling
and Washington waste / John J. Kohut ; illustrated by Drew Friedman.
    p. cm.
  Includes bibliographical references.
  ISBN 0-452-27314-5
  1. Waste in government spending—United States. 2. Government purchasing—
United States. 3. Bureaucracy—United States.
  I. Title
HJ2051.K64 1995
336.73—dc20   94-33458
                                                                                CIP

Printed in the United States of America
Set in Century Book and Tekton
Designed by Julian Hamer

Without limiting the rights under copyright reserved above, no part of this
publication may be reproduced, stored in or introduced into a retrieval system,
or transmitted, in any form, or by any means (electronic, mechanical,
photocopying, recording, or otherwise), without the prior written
permission of both the copyright owner and the above publisher of this book.

BOOKS ARE AVAILABLE AT QUANTITY DISCOUNTS WHEN USED TO PROMOTE PRODUCTS OR
SERVICES. FOR INFORMATION PLEASE WRITE TO PREMIUM MARKETING DIVISION, PENGUIN
BOOKS USA INC., 375 HUDSON STREET, NEW YORK, NEW YORK 10014.

To my mom

Acknowledgments

First, thanks to all the reporters and editors who reported these stories in the first place.

Special thanks to my weirdo colleagues Chuck Shepherd and Roland Sweet for sharing their classic clippings along with their encouragement and friendship. Thanks also to my brother Joe for his good words and enthusiasm.

Once again, thanks to Drew Friedman for seeing reality as only he can. Somewhere, Tor Johnson smiles.

As always, thanks to my agent, Gail Ross, for making this project come together and to her assistant, Howard Yoon, for making things work on schedule. Thanks also to my editor, Ed Stackler, for starting me thinking and supporting the result.

Finally, thanks always to 'Lissa.

Contents

Introduction

Consider for a moment just part of the Pentagon's official brownies recipe:

- Pour batter into a pan at a rate that will yield uncoated brownies which, when cut such as to meet the dimension requirements specified in regulation 3.4f, will weigh approximately 35 grams each.
- The dimensions of the coated brownie shall not exceed 3½ inches by 2½ inches by ⅝ inch.
- Shelled walnut pieces shall be of the small piece size classification, shall be of a light color, and shall be U.S. No. 1 of the U.S. Standards for Shelled English Walnuts. A minimum of 90 percent, by weight, of the pieces shall pass through a ⁴⁄₁₆-inch-diameter round-hole screen and not more than 1 percent, by weight, shall pass through a ²⁄₁₆-inch-diameter round-hole screen.

Just like Mom used to make, huh? I'm sure we all have fond memories of Mom hunting around for the ⁴⁄₁₆-inch-diameter round-hole screen at baking time. If you're like me, I'll bet that you're thinking that some folks at the Department of Defense are either (1) wound too tight or (2) have too much time on their hands. Considering the countless examples of such federal rules and regulations that so mangle common sense, it doesn't take much effort to understand why Americans are becoming more outraged, disgruntled, disillusioned with, and downright angry at their government institutions.

Those feelings are mostly directed at two types of government behavior: decision making (which of course leads to policies, rules, regulations, and laws) and the ever-popular spending of our precious tax dollars. As one Sunday morning talking head recently pointed out, "If [candidates for elective office] think they can run on a platform of 'I won't raise your taxes,' they are dead wrong. That's a wash now. Now the public wants to know 'Where will you cut spending?' They really want to know how each and every one of their tax dollars is being spent."

As always my interest in these types of stories begins and ends with my fascination with the limits (or lack thereof) of human behavior and decision-making processes. For those familiar with my previous collections (*News of the Weird, More News of the Weird,* and *Beyond News of the Weird,* coauthored with Chuck Shepherd and Roland Sweet; and *Countdown to the Millennium* and *News from the Fringe,* coauthored with Roland Sweet—all published by Plume) I think you'll recognize these government-related stories as a special subset. While bizarro human behavior in the world at large often occurs in no apparent context (other than that maybe the world really is going to hell in a handbasket or that the year 2000, with all its built-in strangeness, is fast approaching), this collection offers many stories that place strange behavior within the framework of institutionalized weirdness. I recall the story of an official of the Forest Service who admitted that he really required a staff of only nine to do his job but realized that he had better keep his current total of seventeen staffers because "I realized that a government employee who has a staff of only nine doesn't get paid as much as one who has a staff of seventeen." Given the ground rules, why behave in any other manner?

Of course, that context provides only part of the answer. In considering the other half of the story, I have been drawn to the unavoidable conclusion that we are overseen by a vast bureaucratic system peopled by a surprising number of Americans with very strange and different reasoning powers. Why else would they arrive at a twenty-two-page instruction manual for baking a brownie? Just who was it that decided to continue to stockpile helium decades after the demise of our blimp air force? How many people does it take to change a lightbulb at a government nuclear weapons plant? Who built a hospital on an Indian reservation but forgot to equip it with a single telephone?

So, dear reader, the volume you hold in your hands contains several hundred of the strangest, weirdest, funniest, most mind-bending stories of government waste, mismanagement, misjudgment, and misstatements that have fallen into my hands over the years. Remember as you read on, I'm not making this stuff up.

As always, if you've got a clipping that tops mine or just further contributes to this body of evidence, please send it (with the date it appeared and the name of the newspaper) to me at:

Our Wacko Government
P.O. Box 25682
Washington, D.C. 20007

And remember, next November vote early and vote often.

Planet Pentagon

How the Pentagon Makes Fudge Brownies

After 6 months and 175 work hours the Pentagon finally issued its official recipe for fudge brownies. The document, file MIL-C-44072C, is twenty-two pages long. Some of the directions are as follows (verbatim):

- The texture of the brownie shall be firm but not hard.
- Pour batter into a pan at a rate that will yield uncoated brownies which, when cut such as to meet the dimension requirements specified in regulation 3.4f, will weigh approximately 35 grams each.
- The dimensions of the coated brownie shall not exceed 3½ inches by 2½ inches by ⅝ inch.
- Shelled walnut pieces shall be of the small piece size classification, shall be of a light color, and shall be U.S. No. 1 of the U.S. Standards for Shelled English Walnuts. A minimum of 90 percent, by weight, of the pieces shall pass through a 4/16-inch-diameter round-hole screen and not more than 1 percent, by weight, shall pass through a 2/16-inch-diameter round-hole screen.

Pentagon Cooking Hint #52.2747

The following excerpt is from the Department of Defense specifications for determining the proper pumpkin pie filling: "Good consistency means that the canned pumpkin . . . after emptying from the container to a dry-flat surface . . . holds a high mound formation, and at the end of two minutes after emptying on such surface the highest point of the mound is not less than 60 percent of the height of the container."

In 1989 Murray L. Weidenbaum, the first chairman of former President Reagan's Council of Economic Advisers, pointed out that reform of the government procurement office could save $50 billion a year. One example he used to illustrate the bizarre system at work was that the instruction book explaining how a procurement officer should purchase a fruitcake ran fourteen pages long. Among the requirements for acceptable fruitcake was that the presence of vanilla "be organoleptically detected, but not to a pronounced degree." In other words, one should be able to both taste and smell the vanilla in a fruitcake. The specifications further stated: "When the cooled product is bisected vertically and horizontally with a sharp knife it shall not crumble nor [sic] show any compression streaks, gummy centers, soggy areas, be excessively dry or overprocessed."

When You've Got It, Flaunt It, Baby, Flaunt It!

A 1994 report by the General Accounting Office questioned numerous instances of defense contractors' charging the Pentagon for costs related to employee morale. Sparta Inc., a California-based Pentagon computer contractor, billed the government a total of $560,000 for employees' conferences in Maui, Jamaica, Hawaii, Mexico, and Grand Cayman Island. Sippican Inc., of Marion, Massachusetts, a maker of oceanographic gear for the Navy, billed the Pentagon $11,000 for liquor, $62,000 for employees' use of a company-owned forty-six-foot fishing boat, $15,000 for T-shirts, $5,000 for running shoes, $6,000 for Red Sox tickets, and $31,000 for scholarships for employees and their children. Another contractor charged the Pentagon $2,184 for a hospitality suite at the 1991 Tailhook Convention.

How Red Is That Tape?

In the emergency buildup just prior to the Persian Gulf War, the Air Force requested six thousand radio receivers from Motorola. However, since it was a rush job, competitive bidding would not be followed; there was no time. In that case, according to Pentagon regulations, the manufacturer would have to produce records showing that the product was manufactured at the lowest possible price—records so detailed that they would track even the cost of one microchip. Since the company did not have those accounting records on hand, the Air Force was stuck. In order to get the radios to the service while it still needed them, it was decided that the government of Japan would purchase the radios and then donate them to the U.S. Air Force. And Japan got to count the cost of the radios toward its total contribution to the Gulf War.

In That Fine Tradition of Destroying a Village in Order to Save It ...

According to a report in *The New York Times*, Pentagon chief William Perry has advocated continuing to subsidize those parts of the military industry that cannot easily make a transition to peacetime commercial products. This would include such industries as the makers of nuclear submarines, tanks, and fighter jets. For instance, the Pentagon is planning to purchase a third Seawolf sub at a cost of $2.3 billion not because it needs one to patrol the oceans but because the alternative, shutting down the production line only to have to reopen it someday in the future, is likely to be much more costly.

Ghost Riders in the Payroll Line

An investigation by the General Accounting Office revealed that the Department of Defense issued approximately $8 million in unauthorized pay. Some of those receiving the checks included seventy-six deserters who were officially declared AWOL and at least six ghost employees created by four real employees. Senate Governmental Affairs Chairman John Glenn (D., Ohio) said, "I would note with some incredulity that one of these ghosts had a rather good career in the Army. He was deployed to ... Asia and promoted six ranks to sergeant first class." In one case a soldier was due $183.69 in separation pay but was instead issued a check for $836,919.19. The GAO noted that the soldier in question put $100,000 in a savings account, paid off a relative's debt with $200,000, invested $300,000, and gave the rest to charity. The report also said that the Pentagon had between $32 billion and $41 billion in unmatched disbursements—checks that were written but never matched with a bill in the first place. "It's as if you and I paid our credit card bill without first seeing what the charges were for," said Glenn. It was also noted that for the first nine months of fiscal year 1993, Pentagon contractors returned $1.4 billion to the Pentagon in overpayments! Asked Glenn: "How much is owed the government in overpayments that contractors haven't returned?"

Son of the $2,000 Toilet Seat

In early 1994 three whistle-blowers in the U.S. Navy came forward and told the House Armed Services Oversight and Investigations subcommittee that the service was being charged $544.09 for a spark plug connector that was currently available at local hardware stores for $10.77, tax included. Subcommittee Chairman Norman Sisisky (D., Virginia) noted that his investigators were able to locate a retailer for the connector and purchase it in one day. The Pentagon contractor required a five-month delivery period. The connector is used in a drone aircraft which costs $850,000 total.

- Around 1990 it was revealed that the Air Force paid $999.20 for a pair of pliers. Pratt & Whitney, the builder of jet engines, told the Pentagon that the pliers were needed to modify the engines on F-111 aircraft. The contractor hired a subcontractor to build the pliers for $669 each and then added $330.20 in overhead and profit.

That Money Could Have Been Used to Buy Ninety Spark Plug Connectors!

In 1989 Congress directed the Pentagon to spend $49,000 to conduct a survey to determine if members of the armed forces would spend money on a military lottery ticket.

Now If They'd Just Named It the "All-Sunshine/Tentative Attack" Helicopter . . .

In April 1990 the General Accounting Office reported that the Army's $12 billion AH-64A Apache helicopter gunship program was so plagued with maintenance problems that it recommended production be ended. Despite its designation as an "all-weather" helicopter, the Apache regularly broke down because of environmental problems. During the invasion of Panama the helicopter's sensitive electronics, which had to be kept very cool, had water condense all over them in the tropical climate. Apache crews were forced to attempt to dry certain parts on a stove. The parts failure rate during military exercises in Germany forced the manufacturer, the McDonnell Douglas Corporation, to drive around the region dispensing spare parts to grounded maintenance crews. Some parked Apaches were padlocked for fear that other crews would steal parts for their own repair needs. The Apache—a steal at $14 million per helicopter.

So That the Cockroaches Can Communicate with One Another

When Senator Carl Levin (D., Michigan) looked into reports that the Air Force was spending $73 million to purchase 173 custom fax machines designed by Litton Industries to survive nuclear blasts, he found the reports to be inaccurate. Actually, the service was spending $94.6 million—or $547,000 per fax machine. The Air Force had rejected a fax machine built by Magnavox that cost only $15,000 each. That model was built to the required specifications, but it transmitted pages in "newspaper" quality while the Litton model transmitted in "magazine" quality.

Yossarian, Call Your Office!

The Senate Budget Committee determined that during the 1980s Department of Defense efficiency experts saved between $27 million and $136 million each year. However, the work of the efficiency experts cost between $150 million and $300 million each year.

A Country at War with Itself

In 1976 a stray U.S. Army missile from the White Sands Missile Range hit the nearby New Mexico retirement community of Timberton. Three years later the developers filed a $3.7 million damage suit, claiming that sales on the site have been hampered by "susceptibility . . . to missile impact."

- In 1986 Marine Cobra helicopters practicing warfare scenarios over Arizona missed their designated target and instead fired dozens of rounds into a privately owned garage near Yuma, miles from the target site.
- In May 1989 an Air Force F-16 Fighting Falcon dropped a live five-hundred-pound bomb over Brantley, Georgia, narrowly missing several homes. The pilot was returning to base after a training exercise. During the exercise he had tried to release the bomb, but it wouldn't drop. Then, as he got over Brantley, the bomb fell. The live bomb detonated on

impact, but no one was injured. It missed a cluster of fifteen houses by a thousand yards.

- Later that year two U.S. Navy A-6 attack bombers out of El Centro, California, overshot their targets on the Chocolate Mountain Aerial Gunnery Range and dropped a dozen bombs just three hundred yards short of a campsite. As the bombs were dropping, the error was detected and the mission was aborted. One camper was slightly injured by shrapnel. Another of the campers, George Hurley, forty-six, described the bombing as "unreal. It just pulverized the area." The bombing ignited several small fires.

On Not Knowing When to Come In out of the Rain

Male members of the U.S. Army are forbidden to carry umbrellas. We're not talking about in the middle of a jungle or in desert warfare; we're talking about at the Pentagon on a rainy day or in downtown Washington, D.C., or anywhere a uniformed male member of the service may need to walk in the rain. Female Army members can use them. So can everybody in the Air Force and the Navy. As recently as the fall of 1993 the senior officers of the Army once more endorsed the ban.

Once the Government Says You're Dead

Despite protests from his family that it just wasn't enough evidence, the Pentagon went ahead with plans to bury the tooth of Army Warrant Officer Gregory S. Crandall at Arlington National Cemetery and officially declare him as having died during the Vietnam War. The Pentagon says that the tooth, discovered at a crash site in Laos, explains Crandall's death and closes his file. Crandall's family protested that it wasn't enough evidence to address their fears as to his fate since his helicopter crashed in 1971. The Pentagon noted that Crandall's dog tags had been found at the site nine months prior to the tooth's discovery in 1991. The tooth was buried in a full-size steel casket with full military honors. The price of the service was $2,000 and included a headstone for the tooth. The family, not wanting the service to be conducted, attended under protest and sent out an announcement which read: "The family of Warrant Officer Gregory S. Crandall regrets to announce the burial of a single tooth as his remains at Arlington National Cemetery on Sept. 17 at 1 P.M. Your attendance is welcome."

Yeah, but They Got a Killer Football Team

Since 1946 the U.S. Army's School of the Americas at Fort Benning, Georgia, has trained more than 56,000 Latin American soldiers in counterinsurgency skills. Currently budgeted at $3 million annually (part of a $42 million-a-year program to train 4,000 foreign military troops annually), the school is supposed to instill democratic values and a sense of professionalism that the soldiers will take back to their troops. While studying here, the students routinely get free tickets to Atlanta Braves baseball games and free trips to Disney World.

Among the program's shining graduates are:

- 19 of the 27 Salvadoran officers implicated in the 1989 massacre of 6 Jesuit priests at El Salvador's Central American University
- 4 of 5 Honduran officers accused of organizing a secret death squad in their country
- 6 Peruvian officers linked to a death squad that butchered 9 Lima college students
- 105 of the 246 Colombian officers accused of human rights violations at home
- Roberto d'Aubuisson, Class of '72, who managed Salvadoran death squads and ordered assassination of a Catholic bishop while he said mass
- Voted Most Likely to Succeed by Assassinating Rivals and Making Lots of Money in the International Drug Racket: Manuel Noriega, Class of '65

Since 1991 the school has required graduates to take four hours of "mandatory human-rights awareness training." The following is a question on a test given as part of the course:

The squad leader gives an order to cut off the ears of dead enemy soldiers as proof of the number of casualties. You should:

a. Obey the order but denounce it to your superiors.
b. Obey the order.
c. Disobey the order and tell your superiors about the incident.
d. Order a squad member of lower rank to obey the order.

For Lack of a Keystroke, the Battle Was Lost

Since at least 202,000 of the Air Force's 331,000 enlisted personnel must be able to enter data into a computer or perform "keyboard-related tasks," typing is a requirement in this branch of the armed forces. However, an investigation by the Air Force Audit Agency determined that as many as 157,000 of the 202,000 typers have not had formal instruction. This has led to "lowered production rates, increased backlogs for data input, and increased frustration among employees performing jobs without the needed skill."

What? The Big Game's Today? Well, Since We're Already Here ...

When Secretary of the Air Force Donald Rice flew on an Air Force jet with his wife to Notre Dame University on the day of the big game between Notre Dame and Air Force in 1990, the timing was just a coincidence. It must have been because after his office had been alerted to the fact that the taxpayers had footed the $5,700 bill for the ride, Rice's spokesperson explained that the reason he traveled there that day was to discuss "official business" with ROTC cadets at the school.

I Think Pearl Harbor Used to Work on This Schedule

After spending at least $1.05 billion to build the advanced over-the-horizon Backscatter radar system to guard against a Soviet bomber attack, the Air Force announced that it was cutting back on the twenty-four-hour operation of the system just one year after it came on-line. In a cost-saving move it decided to operate the system only forty hours a week. The director of operations, Lieutenant Colonel Marty Zahn, acknowledged that since Cold War tensions had eased anyway, the system was really only being used to detect drug smugglers. Even reduced operations at the site in Bangor, Maine, will cost $19 million per year.

- In a related story *The New York Times* reported that the attempt by the North American Aerospace Defense Command (NORAD) to redirect its radar system to fight drug smuggling has not worked very well. The NORAD radar-carrying balloons can't be sent up in bad weather, jet fighters sent up to scope out suspect planes fly so fast that the pilots can't get a good look at the planes' tailfin identification numbers, and most important, the NORAD radar systems were built to detect high-flying Soviet bombers while drug smugglers often fly low enough to evade such detection. The NORAD commander, Air Force General Charles Horner, also noted, "One thing that's a downer is the realization that very small amounts of total drugs come by air." The cost of the NORAD war on drugs is estimated to be $80 million per year.

- As recently as 1989 the NORAD complex at Cheyenne Mountain, Colorado, was still using antiquated radar monitors from the 1950s to track airplanes, satellites, submarines, and missile launches. The phone which would be used to call the President of the United States to warn him of an imminent nuclear attack was still wired through a plug-in switchboard. If you didn't know that was the case, you can probably rest easier now. A planned $1.3 billion upgrade of the system was to have been completed by 1994.

Deep Six

Around 1960 the Navy removed the nuclear reactor from the submarine *Seawolf* and dropped it off the coast of Delaware in ninety-one hundred feet of water. When it went to look for it twenty years later, it couldn't find it.

- In the late 1970s fishing boats in Block Island Sound were dredging up canisters of classified documents. The documents were traced to the nuclear attack submarine USS *Shark* based in New London, Connecticut. A Navy spokesperson termed the dumpings of documents a "mistake" because "just about everything that has to do with . . . a nuclear submarine is considered classified" but added that the papers "wouldn't give any secrets away, nor would they really be of use to somebody who wasn't familiar with submarines or submarine operations."

Don't Ask, Don't Smell

According to a report by ABC-TV's *Prime Time Live*, two Marine Corps members of the "silent drill team" were injured during a hazing episode in February 1992. During a "Hell Night" graduation ritual at the end of a five-month training program for the drill team, the two marines had human waste, fermented tobacco spit, and dead rodents dumped on them and their genitals were smeared with a shoe polish containing a caustic chemical. "It was the most excruciating pain that I've ever endured," said one. "It felt like somebody was actually burning me. I was hysterical," said the other. "If I . . . did that to a POW, they'd probably court-martial me and put me in Leavenworth for the rest of my life." After reporting the incident, the two were the victims of retaliation: one was assigned to yard and grounds maintenance, and the other was physically attacked by one of his hazers. The two subsequently left the corps. The three marines who conducted the hazing were each fined several hundred dollars and reassigned. A Marine Corps spokesperson called the hazing an "aberration" and said that those involved were "very young, probably 19 and 20." An attorney for the two victims noted that such hazings have gone on for years in the corps and said: "The military has a hard time recognizing criminal conduct. They wouldn't recognize it if it bit them in the butt."

Sorry, Kid ... Now If You Were a Hazer Instead of a Whistle-blower ...

According to reporting in *The Progressive* by writer Tom Alibrani, when seaman Aaron Ahearn came aboard the U.S. Navy's *Abraham Lincoln*, he was assigned to the sewage detail. According to Ahearn's story, he was instructed to dump two hundred plastic bags of garbage into the sea every day. He also was ordered to dump old computers, desks, solvents, and raw sewage. When he tried to photograph the dumpings, an officer threw his camera overboard. A request for a transfer of duties was ripped up in his face. "In six months I saw enough stuff to make anybody who cares about this world throw up," said Ahearn. He went AWOL but then turned himself in a couple of months later. While the Navy denies that it violated its own rules and environmental laws, other former sailors have come forward to attest that they also routinely threw such garbage into the ocean in clear violations of the law. Tried and convicted, Ahearn received thirty-five days in the brig, a reduction of rank, and a $500 fine.

It's Official! Doomsday Canceled!

With the end of the Cold War the Pentagon officially ended its involvement in planning the "Doomsday Project" in October 1994. Born in 1983, when President Reagan signed Security Decision Directive 55, the plan was to create "continuity in government" during a nuclear attack that could last as long as six months. (By the way, one of the drafters of the directive was Colonel Oliver North.) Using a team of two hundred commandos, scores of secret bunkers, and a fleet of sixteen lead-lined tractor-trailer trucks, the system would keep communication links between surviving military and civilian officials during and after a nuclear exchange. According to *The New York Times*, after eleven years and at least $8 billion, the trucks are now stored in Army depots. A former Strategic Air Command officer involved in analyzing the plan told the newspaper that the biggest problem with creating a communications network was secrecy. The Doomsday Project involved as many as twenty different "black programs": highly classified projects whose very existence is known by very few. "That raised the bureaucratic nightmare to the nth power," said the analyst. "No one knew what anyone else was doing. It was hard to find out even the technical characteristics of some of the plans. You had all the difficulties of creating command-and-control networks cutting across bureaucratic lines, combined with the secrecy of black programs—even the bureaucrats running it were handicapped."

Safety First

In the mid 1980s so many soldiers were being run over by tanks and other Army vehicles while they slept that the service launched a major safety campaign to put an end to the accidents. Between March 25, 1984, and October 28, 1986, twenty-two sleeping soldiers on field training exercises were run over in nineteen separate accidents by other soldiers driving Army vehicles. The report said that the soldiers were sleeping where they shouldn't have been and that the drivers involved failed to send out crew members as walking guides. The safety campaign urged tough disciplinary action in future cases and suggested a new education program to teach soldiers a set of hand motions recognizable by drivers. (I can think of one.)

Orange Crush

In 1988 Army Dr. Michael Cosio of the Walter Reed Army Medical Center in Washington, D.C., published a study in the *Journal of the American Medical Association* on the dangers of falling soda machines. Cosio reviewed fifteen cases all involving males at U.S. military installations abroad between July 1985 and September 1987. Three of the victims were killed, and twelve were hospitalized. The machines fell because the soldiers, either trying to get their change back or hoping for a free drink, rocked the machines vigorously back and forth. Cosio also looked at thirty-two more cases, some involving civilians, in which eight more people were killed by the machines. Wrote Cosio: "In essence, each victim said, 'It came down faster than I thought. I pushed up, but it was too heavy and it kept coming. I tried to get out of the way but it caught me.'" Each soda machine weighs between eight hundred pounds and one thousand pounds. Cosio, urging that the machines be anchored so that they can't tip over, said, "If they get hurt if a machine lands on them, they have a 20 percent to 25 percent chance that they get killed."

- Several months before Cosio's report was released, the U.S. Army Safety Center produced a study of fifty-two vending machine accidents involving military personnel. The recommendation of the study was to outfit all vending machines with a decal showing a pictograph of a machine falling onto a man.

I Know! They Can Teach Them How to Get Their Money Back from a Vending Machine

According to reporting by *The Progressive*, the U.S. Army has a plan to "support local [school] districts in offering at-risk youth a new opportunity to be successful in school and thus in life" by doubling the number of high schools nationwide that currently offer Junior ROTC programs from fifteen hundred to three thousand by the year 1997. In July 1993 the Reserve Officers Training Corps (ROTC) Cadet Command at Fort Monroe, Virginia, released its outline of the program that would also establish "career academies" at certain "target schools" that would have all ROTC students spending their whole day together in a group and having all their normal high school courses taught by military retirees. By the way, the Navy, Air Force, and Marines have similar plans for ROTC programs in the works.

Why the Military Shouldn't Be Fighting in the War on Drugs

In the midst of the Panama invasion in 1989 a U.S. Army infantry task force searching a house frequented by Panamanian strongman General Manuel Noriega reported that they found five pounds of cocaine there. Actually Noriega's Brazilian sorceress lived in the house, and it was the site of numerous black magic rituals in which the general was involved. The Army task force said that the cocaine was found wrapped in banana leaves and stored in a freezer. "We're sure it's cocaine," said the commander in charge. U.S. forces believed that this was even more proof of Noriega's involvement in the drug trade. However, a further investigation by the Army's Criminal Investigation Division determined that the banana leaves were actually tamales that the sorceress used in her magic rituals to cast curses on Noriega's enemies. In fact, when the CID agents looked into the tamales, they found pieces of paper inside each one with the name of a Noriega opponent written on them.

Advanced Accounting 101: Prof. Westmoreland

According to a House Armed Services Committee report, the U.S. Army failed at its task of assessing Iraqi armor losses during the air attack phase of the Gulf War because "the army had little idea of how to do this. There simply was—and is—no book, no doctrine" on how to assess battle damage. Oversight and Investigations Subcommittee Chairman Representative Norman Sisisky (D., Virginia) noted that the Army kept changing its methodology throughout the six-week air campaign but still produced "astoundingly exaggerated" data. Their damage reports were to be the basis on which it would be decided when to start the ground war. The Army report estimated that 388 of the 846 Iraqi Republican Guard tanks were destroyed prior to the start of the ground war. A later analysis of spy plane photos during the same period showed that no more than 215 and possibly as few as 166 of the tanks were actually destroyed.

And They Told You Playing Army as a Kid Was a Waste of Time

Thirty-one employees of the defense-consulting firm BDM International, Inc. work as citizens of the fictional third-world nation of Cortina, located at Fort Chaffee, Arkansas. About five thousand U.S. infantry troops come through Cortina each year to do battle with a fictional rebel army played by an U.S. Army infantry regiment. The BDM employees portray police, army, and civilian officials as well as other citizenry of the country. The exercise is supposed to prepare American personnel for action in underdeveloped countries where they will have a close interaction with the civilian population. All players in the exercise are outfitted with laser sensors, and those armed carry laser-equipped guns so that when anyone is shot, a sensor goes off. The BDM employees spend their days staging demonstrations, blockading roads, enacting village scenes such as marriage ceremonies, and generally "playing army" with the troops.

Anchors Away

In 1990, following weeks of controversy at the U.S. Naval Academy during which there were allegations of cheating on exams and the hazing of a coed who was chained to a urinal, the graduates of the academy were presented diplomas showing that they had graduated from the "Navel Academy." The error, made by a printing company, was discovered too late to be corrected by the time of the commencement ceremonies.

We Could Go Back to My Place and Look at My Training Posters

A senior Navy officer on the faculty of the Naval War College was forced to submit his resignation after a Navy investigation showed that he asked female Navy civilian employees to pose nude for photographs that he said would be used for a series of training posters on board ships deployed in the Persian Gulf. The captain sent one woman a letter proposing that she "work with [him] on a fun but outrageous project." The letter went on to suggest that "a cleaning sequence could move from routine deck scrubbing to a wet t-shirt then even more revealing poses. A favorite of several wives was a housecleaning, laundry, kitchen work sequence designed to emphasize their hard work at home." It also said that the photos would be used as training posters on "ship safety, security, fitness, nutrition, proper procedures, communications as well as remembering loved ones at home" and were destined for ships deployed as part of Operation Desert Shield. A naval investigation said that the captain's photo taking was "an unofficial venture" that he took on "personally." It was determined that he had photographed at least ten other women over several years and that some of the photo sessions had taken place in a classroom submarine trainer. The captain was charged with conduct unbecoming an officer and fined $1,000. It was suggested that he resign, and he did.

Free Flipper!

In the 1992 Defense Appropriations Act Congress instructed the Department of Defense to "develop training procedures which will allow mammals which are no longer required for this project to be released into their natural habitat." About $550,000 was earmarked for the task. The mammals in question are one hundred dolphins, twenty sea lions, and a few belugas and "false killer" whales. The "project" they are no longer needed for began in 1960, ran through the 1970s and 1980s, and cost an estimated $8 million per year. It involved Navy programs to teach the mammals to fetch objects underwater, serve as underwater guards at ports, and escort ships at sea as mine hunters. Now the hundred dolphins and the other sea creatures sit in holding pens at the San Diego Naval Ocean Systems Center. The $550,000 to study a release process was used up in one two-day meeting of specialists in Albuquerque, New Mexico, in

June 1992. The report by the experts doubts that dolphins held longer than seven years could be reintroduced successfully into the wild. Animal rights groups countered that dolphins that have escaped the program over the years have readapted and survived in the wild. Meanwhile, the dolphins sit in cages eight yards long and eight yards wide.

Great Futures Await in the Insurance Industry

The House Armed Services Oversight and Investigations Subcommittee released a report early in 1994 critical of the Navy's investigations of reported suicides among its sailors. The report charged that the service fails to follow standard law enforcement procedures and regularly withholds information from next of kin on their investigations. At least seventy families complained about the conduct of Navy investigators in the suicide investigations of relatives. In one case a Navy investigator went to the parents of a twenty-two-year-old lance corporal found shot to death and told them that he had killed himself in a game of Russian roulette. Later the same day the investigator returned to the parents' home and said that their son had actually died cleaning his rifle. The following day he returned to say that their son was killed "playing" with his rifle and had shot himself in the left temple, not under the chin, as he had previously informed them. Later the parents found out that their son had been shot in the right temple. In another case ruled a suicide, a sailor on board the USS *Virginia* was found strangled by a telephone cord wrapped twice around his neck, and both his wallet and diary were missing. In yet another case a marine was found near Camp Lejeune with a rifle shot in his head and a shotgun blast in his chest. His finger was still wrapped around the rifle trigger, but the shotgun was found eight to ten feet away. It was ruled a suicide. Further fuel was added to the complaints by the families when a *Philadelphia Inquirer* investigation quoted former military investigators as charging that suicide is the routine designation for crimes the military tries to hide. Still, the House subcommittee report concluded that the Navy "does not have a policy, campaign, conspiracy or predisposition to present homicides as suicides."

The Ugly Construction Worker

A General Accounting Office report on the Pentagon's Humanitarian and Civic Assistance Program concluded that the various construction projects undertaken by the program failed to "improve the local populations' work skills" and often left foreign communities with a poor impression of American aid. In Panama a new hospital roof constructed by U.S. troops under the auspices of the program was built with an inward slant, thus leaving the clinic flooded during the rain season. The GAO said that a Honduran road project was so bungled that it left the Hondurans with the perception that the United States builds "only half roads."

It's Not Easy Being Green

The Pentagon's recycling program, begun in 1982, was supposed to cut down on waste by allowing military base commanders to sell recyclable materials. The money earned from the program was supposed to pay for the program and environmental projects, with any leftover funds going to the base morale, welfare, and recreation (MWR) fund. A General Accounting Office report determined that among the items being sold through the program are such nonrecyclable materials as jet engines, aircraft parts, and containers of oil and solvents. The agency concluded that because the bases were selling these items, "millions of dollars are being used annually for MWR activities that should be used instead to offset the need for appropriated funds or be returned to the U.S. Treasury." According to a report by Jack Anderson, one Army base used $250,000 of the funds to build a fishing pond and firearms range while spending less than half that on environmental projects.

- As of 1994 the Pentagon said that eleven thousand of its properties in this country are polluted, and one estimate says the cleanup costs could amount to $35 billion. According to a report by *The Philadelphia Inquirer*, environmental cleaning projects at sites owned by the departments of Energy and Defense are the fastest-growing part of the federal budget.

What a Loss

Under pressure from the German government, U.S. officials finally decided in 1992 to stop selling copies of Hitler's *Mein Kampf* in military bookstores in Germany. The 150 such bookstores in Germany are run by *Stars and Stripes*, the U.S. military newspaper. German Foreign Ministry officials charged that the United States was ignoring German laws restricting the sale of the book in their country and was in violation of the German copyright. *Stars and Stripes* said that it had sold about a thousand copies a year.

Forget Them! What About the Amway Practitioners?

In order to deal with the presence of different religious views among U.S. military personnel, in the 1980s Kirschner Associates was paid $30,000 by the Pentagon to provide military chaplains with instructions on how best to minister to personnel who belong to unconventional religions, such as the Council of Witches, Pagans, Wiccans, or the Church of Satan.

This Answers a Lot of Questions

Every Friday morning the Pentagon Meditation Club meets in a windowless room deep in the complex to discuss inner peace, world peace, and meditation. Members of the group say that they are trying to establish a "peace shield" around planet Earth by means of their meditation practices. They call this their "Spiritual Defense Initiative." The group, which numbers about eighty, was established in 1976 by now-retired Air Force Captain Edward Winchester. It was first known as the TM Club, for transcendental meditation. Winchester believes that each person has a "peace shield" or natural aura and that it can be measured by means of a "peace shield gauge," which the club sells for $65 each. According to one member, "Meditation can exert some psychic influence on people and world events."

If You Still Doubt That Cable Has Changed Everything . . .

Since 1991 the Defense Intelligence Agency has been broadcasting a television show on the Defense Intelligence Network, a Pentagon version of CNN available to an audience of only about a thousand intelligence and operations officers at the Pentagon and at nineteen other sites in the United States who hold the credentials to be informed on highly classified information. For twelve hours a day, five days a week, the DIN broadcasts reports assessments and early warnings of the world's trouble spots. "In the upper corner of the screen, we put the classification of the actual document or what is being said, and that can change every twenty seconds," said one official. The program, known officially as the Joint Worldwide Intelligence Communications System, features at least seven different anchors. The broadcast lineup includes a 6:45 A.M. show that interviews visiting intelligence briefers, the *Regional Intelligence Review*, *Military Trends and Capabilities* show, and *Global Update*, which appears at the top of each hour.

Before You Resume the Torture, How About Those Knicks, Huh?

During the Persian Gulf War the U.S. Central Command issued all troops a fifty-page *Troop Information Handbook* designed in part to foster understanding of Arab culture. A report in the *National Journal* highlighted some of the handy information contained in the handbook. For instance, readers learned that hand-holding between Arab men "indicates nothing more than the fact that they are good friends." Troops were also warned against offering a Muslim "Liquor or pork, bacon, pork & beans, lard, bacon bits [or] pig's feet." Among conversation topics to be avoided were comments about the "Jewish Lobby" and an Arab boycott of "companies which have strong Zionist representation." It also included the fail-safe advice of: "Don't be too arrogant, too generous, too smart, too patronizing, etc." And in case one was captured and held hostage, he or she was advised to "discuss only neutral issues such as sports."

Make the Stars, and They Will Come

Despite the paucity of five-star generals, the Defense Logistical Agency in one instance estimated that it would need 2,500 sets of five-star insignia bars in addition to the 180 sets it had in storage. This was at a time in the 1980s when there were no living five-star generals at all.

Okay, Fair Is Fair. Now All Taxpayers Get Medals, Too!

During the Gulf War the Navy and Marine Corps' Combat Action Ribbon was given to every crew member aboard thirty ships anywhere near the region, whether the ships saw any combat or not. (In fact, overall the Pentagon was reported to have awarded about four million National Defense Service Medals for participation in Desert Shield and Desert Storm despite the fact that only about half a million troops served in the conflict.) The controversy over this awards methodology both inside and outside the military led the Navy and Marines to change eligibility requirements for those serving in the Somalia operation. The Navy ruled that "personnel [in Somalia] subjected to random sniper, rocket, mortar, etc., fire are not eligible" for the Combat Action Ribbon. The Marine Corps stated that only those marines in Somalia who "participated in retaliatory offensive actions" are eligible.

At Least They Weren't on Their Way to the Golf Course ... Right?

The Washington Post reported in 1994 that for years senior Pentagon officers have regularly traveled from the Pentagon to Andrews Air Force Base in Maryland by helicopter, at a cost of $1,000 to $3,000 per trip. The cab fare for the same journey is $22 and takes about twenty minutes. According to the *Post* report, during 1993 Pentagon officers took 238 such trips. The Pentagon defended the practice, explaining that these people were on busy schedules and were responsible for managing the armed forces. The spokesperson for one of the frequent fliers said that his boss favors helicopters over cars because he travels with "classified material that needs the security" of traveling by air.

Mr. Science Gets Government Funding

Excuse Me!

In 1994 the Environmental Protection Agency gave a $500,000 grant to Utah State University to study the question of whether the burping done by cattle contains enough methane to add to the problem of global warming. Researchers fitted rangeland cattle with special breathing devices to measure the amounts of methane in their burps. In 1991 the government spent $300,000 to look into the question of whether the methane in bovine flatulence was affecting the atmosphere.

Yeah, but Maybe It's Just Nervous Eating

In a planned study for 1994 a team of U.S. and New Zealand scientists will join in an effort to determine why Antarctica's penguins are gaining weight. The fear is that it's just more evidence of the greenhouse effect: If the atmosphere is trapping more heat, then the water in Antarctica is warming and fostering the growth of krill, penguins' primary food source. In order to figure it all out, every morning for three months the team will weigh about three hundred penguins immediately after they have fed. Then, after the penguins regurgitate their food for their young, they'll be weighed again. It is said that the difference in weights will measure the krill population.

Radical New Ideas

According to a joint report by the National Highway Traffic Safety Administration and the Centers for Disease Control, more than one third of the 5,546 pedestrians killed by cars in 1992 had blood alcohol levels higher than the legal limit for driving a motor vehicle. Said a NHTSA spokesman: "This is a bigger problem than we had thought previously.... We have not really addressed the drinking-and-walking issue." Therefore, the agency will spend $370,000 to conduct a study in Baltimore to find out what happens when drunk walkers are hit by cars. "There are a number of potential solutions to this that can't be decided by somebody sitting in Washington," said the official.

So, Two Australians Walk into a Bar . . .

In search of the answer to the question, How many drinks per day does it take to damage your brain?, the U.S. National Institutes of Health (NIH) turned to Australia as ground zero for its research effort. A $500,000 grant to the University of Sydney's pathology department will be used in a three-year effort to study tissue from sixty dissected brains. The study will compare the brains of alcoholics with those of moderate drinkers and teetotalers. "We probably have the highest incidence in the world of Wernicke-Korsakoff syndrome, which results in brain shrinkage as a result of alcoholism," said

Clive Harper, a neuropathologist at the university. "For some reason that nobody has ever satisfactorily explained, Australia has a very high level of brain damage due to alcohol," said Dr. Alex Wodack, a member of the Royal Australian College of Physicians. The NIH has targeted Australia because for some reason Australian drinkers are loyal to their drug of choice and are far less likely than Americans to abuse other drugs.

Crash Test Dummies

Since the 1970s researchers at Heidelberg University in Germany have used more than two hundred human cadavers, including those of children, in automobile crash tests. The tests were commissioned by the German auto industry to judge the effects of crashes on the human body. Faced with criticism in the press when this story leaked out, the university said that it had permission from next of kin for every body used and had special permission from parents to use their children's dead bodies. In the following days it was revealed that the U.S. government had financed some of the Heidelberg research, as well as tests at the University of Virginia and the Medical College of Wisconsin, which also used cadavers in crash tests. George Parker of the National Highway Traffic Safety Administration said that such testing was necessary for improving safety. Other sponsors of the research in the United States included the Ford Motor Company and General Motors Corporation.

Eat it! Tastes Like Chicken

Working with African scientists under a grant from the U.S. Agency for International Development (AID), University of Wisconsin researchers experimented with raising rats in captivity as a food source. In Africa wild rats, which can grow to three or four pounds in weight, are widely sold at markets. Tom Yuill, associate dean of the school of medicine at the university, said that the effort was part of growing experiments in the area of "microlivestock," small animals that can be easily raised in captivity. (Personal note: You know, in a world where the Indian city of New Delhi employs "night rat killers" [whose job it is to go out each night and beat the ever-growing rat population to death] and where each major metropolitan area in the United States has a "rodent control" office, perhaps U.S. AID should save its money and the Commerce Department should get involved in this as an import/export problem. Microlivestock, indeed. Just a thought.)

On Thinking Too Much

According to the publication *EPA Watch*, the Environmental Protection Agency launched a new study in 1993 into the dangers of breathing while you take a shower— specifically, whether one might be injured by inhaling water vapor while washing.

Okay, This Is Going to Be Really Important One Day, and I'm Going to Look Stupid ...

A study undertaken at the genetics department at the University of Washington in Seattle is investigating irregularity among worms. Scientists observing the one-millimeter-long worms defecating are also monitoring a mutant strain they created which is constipated. Funded with U.S. government–certified tax dollars? You betcha.

Thanksgiving on the Red Planet

To the tune of $200,000, NASA has funded the development of a sweet potato that can be grown in outer space.

But Mr. Green Jeans Always Knew When to Water Plants

For more than four years researchers at the United States Department of Agriculture used very sophisticated electronic sound-monitoring devices in an attempt to hear the noises made as a plant's cell structure deteriorated because of a lack of water. The noise of the plants "crying" is in the extremely high-frequency range of one hundred kilohertz, far above the range of human ears. "The sounds are produced when the tension that pulls water from the roots to the leaves increases as drought intensifies," said one scientist. The researchers said that they hoped their work would one day lead to helping farmers improve watering schedules for crops.

I Bet They Loved It!

In 1990 the Air Force paid University of Florida researchers $100,000 to find out if the noise of low-flying F-4 Phantom fighter jets adversely affected pregnant horses living near air bases in the Southwest. In an attempt to replicate the experience, the researchers forced eight pregnant horses to listen to simulated noise blasted directly into their barns. A control group of eight pregnant horses was not exposed to the noise. When last heard from, the veterinarian in charge of the project planned to pursue the research using real jets the following year.

The Ray Guns? I Think Henderson Took Those Home

A Government Accounting Office report released in July 1991 found that the Livermore, Los Alamos, and Lawrence Berkeley national laboratories, all operated by the University of California, had inadequately controlled government property and government documents in their charge. The report found that Livermore couldn't find 16 percent of the government property that was supposedly in its possession. The lab was missing ten thousand of six hundred thousand classified documents, including plans for lasers and nuclear weapons. Another GAO report charged that Livermore paid $590,000 more to lease fifty-eight vehicles from the University of California than it would have been charged to rent the same cars from the General Services Administration.

Can You Make Me a Starship Enterprise? With the Blinking Lights up on the Bridge?

An employee of a Department of Energy (DOE) operation at Rocky Flats, Colorado, revealed in congressional testimony in 1987 that his shop, which was supposed to design and create models of such things as nuclear devices for the national laboratories, was instead regularly instructed by DOE and Livermore lab officials to create specialty items including wine presses, commemorative medals, retirement plaques, gold-plated jewelry, clocks, foot massagers, and paperweights. The witness said that the shop spent at least 30 percent of its time on such projects.

Something Tells Me That the Brainier Scientists Knew the Outcome of This One Before They Started

In 1990 the Department of Energy began a $22 million project to deal with the remains of radiation experiments conducted for the government on the University of California campus at Davis. The first part of the task was the removal of the corpses of 828 beagles that had been stored in freezers at the school. Those dogs were among the 3,700 killed in a twenty-seven-year program to determine the effects of radioactive fallout. The test subjects were fed radioactive food and then were monitored to see how long they'd live. The last beagle died at age eighteen and one-half in 1986. The government paid the university at least $65 million for the work. The bodies were shipped in fifty-five-gallon drums to the Hanford nuclear reservation in Washington State. The shipment of bodies was followed by a shipment of 17.5 tons of their radioactive feces and urine, which had also been stored at Davis.

News Flash! If You Get Shot in the Head, You're in Trouble!

In 1990 the Physicians Committee for Responsible Medicine asked the Pentagon to halt a research program at the Louisiana State University Medical Center in New Orleans. The government-funded project, designed to improve treatment for soldiers whose heads had been injured on the field of battle and return them to duty, involved firing pellets into the heads of anesthesized cats and studying their wounds. The committee said that the $2 million study, sponsored by the Army, was "superfluous and extraordinarily expensive." At least 700 cats were killed during the seven-year project. Describing the procedure, Louisiana Representative Bob Livingston said the scientist in charge "meticulously drilled holes, small holes, in cats' skulls, placed their heads in a vise, and shot BB pellets into their brains." Of the 700 shot, 103 were killed outright. The others were kept brain-wounded but alive so that neurological tests could be conducted. Some wounded cats were forced to walk on balance beams. Dr. Michael Sukoff, spokesman for the Physicians Committee, noted that after seven years of cat shootings the researchers "concluded that a brain-injured organism will stop breathing." The same scientist in charge went on to win a $1.8 million Pentagon contract to study head injuries in rats for five years. (In a separate fourteen-year study at the University of Cincinnati, also paid for by the federal government, live cats were shot in the head with .22-caliber cartridges again in an effort to simulate human head wounds. The university responded to animal rights protestors in 1988 that it hoped the research would offer hope "for restoring injured citizens to productive lives.") According to reporting in *The Village Voice* by Judith Reitman in 1994, the Pentagon spends "about $110 million annually" to kill "more than 500,000 animals a year" in a variety of research projects.

The Rabbit's Holding, Man

In 1993 the Physicians Committee for Responsible Medicine termed "outlandish" a $3 million federally funded research project to determine whether marijuana will make rabbits more susceptible to syphilis and mice more prone to contract Legionnaires' disease.

White or Dark?

In an attempt to study how well the canopies of jet aircraft will hold up after a midair collision with a bird, the Air Force developed the "birdstrike simulator," also known as the chicken gun. Using a converted twenty-foot cannon, four-pound chickens (dead ones) are shot at a speed of 700 mph into a parked plane's windshield to determine the probable extent of such damage in flight. Explaining the chicken gun in a press release in 1983, the Air Force said that "experiments with water bags and other devices simulating birds proved unsatisfactory." In 1982 alone 2,322 Navy and Air Force jets were hit by birds, causing $15 million in damages.

The Government Wants to Make Sure You Know the Following:

The U.S. Centers for Disease Control reported the findings of a study, conducted by the Department of Environmental Health and Natural Resources in North Carolina in 1992, that almost 40 percent of the people killed in falls from horses had been drinking. The study, which examined the blood alcohol content of thirteen persons killed in North Carolina between 1979 and 1989 who had fallen from their horses, discovered that five had been drinking. On the basis of these findings, the CDC wants you to know that drinking and horseback riding don't mix.

Don't Ride and Lick Toads Either

A research ecologist at the Department of the Interior said in 1994 that the practice of "toad licking" as a means of achieving an hallucinogenic "high" is on the decline as the result of the presence of poisonous chemical compounds in the toad venom. However, he reported that "toad-smoking, on the other hand, seems to be less risky and is on the rise."

The Regulators: We're Here to Help!

Streamlining

When a dispute arose over the question of how the Pantex nuclear weapons plant near Amarillo, Texas, would dispose of its nuclear bombs, United States Energy Secretary Hazel O'Leary decided on a course of action that required her to name a six-member committee. That committee then chose a sixteen-member committee. That committee was charged with selecting a committee of eight. According to the plan, those eight added twelve members to their ranks. The final twenty-member committee decided the future of the plant.

What's in a Nickname?

A federal grand jury indicted Roger Halvorson, fifty-six, a meat inspector for the U.S. Department of Agriculture, on three counts of conversion of property. According to the prosecutor, the inspector took prime ribs from

Westlund's Meat Company in Minneapolis, Minnesota, during regular Saturday inspections of the plant over a period of two months. Halvorson, known to plant employees as "Pockets," allegedly slipped the meat into large inside pockets in his trench coat. He then reportedly sold the meat to bars and restaurants.

Few Knew Just How Close This Country Came to Destruction

In 1987 the U.S. Bureau of Alcohol, Tobacco, and Firearms (BATF) banned imports of Collio wines from Italy because the winery's label featured a bosomy naked woman. "The breasts on this label were upthrust and very evident," said Dot Koester, spokesperson for the BATF. "If the picture had been a masterpiece, then it would have been allowed, but it wasn't, so it's obscene." Collio responded by painting over the breasts with gold-leaf paint on four thousand bottles, to create what the company described as a "low-cut, modern swimming costume." A BATF inspector approved the import of those bottles. Months later the winery's bottles destined for this country featured the naked woman minus any breasts. "There is nothing basically objectionable about being perfectly flat-chested," said Koester. "The label is like seeing a man at the beach."

Irwin Corey, Call Your Office

In the hopes of educating computer security professionals, the Treasury Department made available on its Automated Information System computer bulletin board the inner workings of a number of destructive computer viruses. Included were such titles as "The Internet Worm," "Satan's Little Helper," and "Dark Avenger's Mutation Engine," all designed to wreak havoc with information systems. Besides the viruses, the helpful folks at Treasury also made available the "cracker software" used by computer hackers to break access codes and "war dialers," the software used to dial numbers until it finds and records computer lines. One hopes some security professionals looked at the data because the board, operated by the Bureau of Public Debt, is open to anyone who dials into it. So for more than a year any user had access to each of the viruses. According to some critics, even an amateur could use the information provided to develop new strains of virus. The department admitted that it had little information on who dialed into the system and what they looked at or downloaded. All they do know is that at least a thousand computer users dialed into the board while the data were available. The information was withdrawn only after complaints from "anonymous whistle-blowers."

It's the New Mother Nature Takin' Over ...

Back during the 1980s the Bureau of Land Management launched a large-scale intervention effort to preserve Mojave Desert tortoises. When BLM biologists determined that ravens were responsible for 85 percent of the deaths of young tortoises, they decided to start killing ravens. They targeted particularly busy birds who were found to have "hundreds" of turtle shells next to their nests. At the first intervention site the BLM began feeding the ravens hard-boiled eggs to get them used to the food and then began lacing subsequent eggs with poison. To ensure that nobody else ate the eggs, they were wired to platforms near the nests, and each was removed at night. The ravens not poisoned were shot. When finished, the plan was to have killed fifteen hundred of the desert raven population of ten thousand.

Quick! Call President Truman!

It took the Federal Trade Commission until late 1993 to decide that it would no longer attempt the regulation of makers of fallout shelters and home radiation-monitoring devices. An FTC spokesperson called the items "really obsolete." In 1992 the commission asked for public comment on whether existing regulations on these products were still necessary. The request got only one response. Robert Gallagher, president of Nuclear Sources and Services Inc., of Houston, replied, "You couldn't sell a fallout shelter or a radiation instrument to the public if you promised immortality in your advertising."

Honey! That Rat's Making Faces at Us!

Former Senator Malcolm Wallop (R., Wyoming) charged that the Fish and Wildlife Service, in its efforts to protect an endangered rat species, prevented many Southern Californians from properly protecting their homes from wildfires. In its efforts to save the Stephens' kangaroo rat (*Dipodomys stephenssi*), the service warned homeowners near the rats' habitat that they could not build firebreaks on their land because that procedure would destroy the underground burrows where the rats lived. Letters to residents threatened "state and federal prosecution" and warned homeowners not to annoy the rat "to such an extent as to significantly disrupt normal behavioral patterns which include ... breeding, feeding or sheltering." When wildfires ravaged the area in October 1993, a Wallop spokesperson noted, the homes that ignored the warning and built the traditional firebreaks survived. Said Wallop, the Endangered Species Act "does not require them [the Fish and Wildlife Service people] to be idiots." Despite the anecdotal evidence, a GAO report released in 1994 said that county officials and fire experts at the scene found homes with and without the firebreaks were destroyed. It concluded that the Fish and Wildlife policy was not to blame.

They Can Take My Electric Worm Probe When They Pry It out of My Cold, Dead Fingers

In 1993 the Consumer Product Safety Commission formally announced the recall of eighty-three thousand electric worm probes. The hand-held devices, which send an electrical current into the ground to shock worms and force them to the surface, have been used by fishing enthusiasts for years. The commission determined that the probes have killed more than thirty people since 1973. Users who touch metal surfaces or stand on wet ground while using the devices are susceptible to shock. Critics noted that the agency issued previous recalls of the probes in 1976 and 1988 but that neither effort stopped manufacturers from producing the dangerous tools. Said a spokesman for the commission: "We try to cover the products with the most deaths and injuries. A product with 30 deaths since 1973 is a concern, but it's not at the top of the list."

NASA: No Alternative Space Agency

For That Price It'd Better ... Oh, Forget It

In 1993 the General Accounting Office criticized NASA for the costs involved in building a prototype toilet for the space shuttle. The $23 million price tag was the result of a 900 percent price increase resulting from design changes. NASA said that the manufacturer, United Technologies Hamilton Standard, was forced into cost increases when astronauts requested that a manual flush be substituted for an automatic feature. While it cost $23 million to make, a fully operational model would cost an additional $7 million. In its first test aboard the shuttle *Endeavor* in 1993, mission control had to remind the astronauts to keep the toilet lid down when it wasn't in use. When sensors indicated that the device's fans and airflow were operational even though no one was sitting on it, the ground controller told the crew "to make sure that the lid is closed and the fan cycles off, if you could remember."

How About "Sex"?

After the old space station Freedom project rose from its own ashes as a new multibillion-dollar "international" project, NASA requested in late 1993 that the public submit proposals for a new name. The agency suggested that the name for the joint effort of the U.S. and Russian space agencies (which will also involve the Japanese, the Canadians, and the European Space Agency) reflect the new era of cooperation. The requirements were that the name be simple, easily pronounced, not an acronym, not the name of a living person, not a name already used, possess worldwide meaning, and be easily translatable to other languages.

The Phantom Knows

NASA flew a human skull fitted with 125 radiation sensors aboard three shuttle flights in 1989 and 1990. As part of an effort to find out what radiation hazards astronauts face in outer space, the skull was cut into pieces and rearranged around the radiation detectors. It was then covered with a substance simulating human flesh and facial features. A NASA medical expert said that the skull was from a person who had willed his or her body to science. "I have no idea whether it was from someone in this country. I understand skeletons for medical experimentation often come from other countries, the Philippines and so forth." The skull's official NASA designation is the "phantom."

- *Star Trek* creator Gene Roddenberry's widow disclosed in 1994 that sometime after his death his ashes were taken into space aboard a space shuttle mission and then brought back down to Earth. It was later revealed that the ashes flew as the personal effects of mission commander James Wetherbee on board a shuttle *Columbia* mission in October 1992. It was Roddenberry's last wish.

We Put Some Decals on the Side, Too! Looks Cool!

A NASA contractor used a superstrength glue, like the kind commercially available in model shops, for six years to make unauthorized repairs on space shuttle engines. A NASA deputy manager said that dabs of the superglue were used to fix a pump in the main engines of the craft but did not pose a hazard. However, the problem was that no company officials or NASA officials knew of the repairs. "That's the bad part of it. It was an unauthorized repair, and the management of this company did not realize what was going on. That's been corrected," said the NASA official. The glue was used to attach thin silver plating to tabs on the pumps. It was discovered only when inspectors noticed its not holding in one case. Then the engineers decided that the silver plating wasn't needed to begin with and ordered it removed from all the pumps.

Pay No Attention to
the Man Behind the Curtain!

Former Representative Howard Wolpe (D., Michigan), said that congressional investigators looking into a NASA program to design nuclear reactors to power space vehicles stumbled upon an agency memo instructing employees on how to deal with requests filed under the Freedom of Information Act (FOIA). In a letter to NASA Administrator Richard Truly, Wolpe charged that the document instructed government employees to "rewrite and even destroy documents 'to minimize adverse impact,' " to "mix up documents and camouflage handwriting so that the document's significance would be 'less meaningful,' " and "to 'enhance the utility' of various FOIA exemptions." A NASA lawyer said that the document in question was "a misrepresentation."

It's All in the Timing

The Hubble space telescope was launched into orbit on April 24, 1990. In June NASA scientists discovered that the telescope's ninety-four-inch primary mirror had an optical defect that caused somewhat blurred vision. The repair plan devised later that year and finally carried out in 1993 cost about $86 million. Prior to its launch the Hubble had sat in a warehouse for quite some time. If the optical defect had been discovered while it was still on the ground, repair costs would have been about $2 million. On top of that, the actual error had occurred ten years earlier, when technicians building the telescope tried to fill a gap in an optical testing device they were using with three small washers. The cost of the washers? Twenty-five cents each.

Whoops!

In August 1993 NASA lost contact with the $980 million *Mars Observer*. The craft, designed to photograph the Red Planet, was 450 million miles out and about to go into its planned orbit when ground controllers could get no response from it. An independent panel investigating the disaster months later concluded that the problem was most likely a failure in the craft's propulsion system. However, *The Washington Post* reported in early 1994 that seven months prior to the launch of the *Observer*, NASA managers made a decision that may have played a role in the mission failure. The original plan for the craft called for its propellant tanks to be pressurized five days after the launch. Instead NASA decided to delay pressurization for eleven months until the *Observer* was about to go into Mars orbit. While the decision was designed to avoid a leak, the valves involved were not designed to operate under the different conditions. Sources quoted by the newspaper suggested that the delay may have caused an even greater leak than feared and ruptured the craft's fuel line. When the independent panel gave its report to the press, no mention of the delayed pressurization was made. The chairman of that panel, asked later about the omission, said that "it was an oversight." According to the newspaper, the procedural change is mentioned twice in the four-volume report, but those volumes were available for review only at NASA headquarters.

Volume 23 in the Continuing History of Coincidence

A report by NASA's inspector general revealed that space shuttle astronauts used their two-seater supersonic training jets, in which they are required to log fifteen hours of flight time each month, to fly ten- to twelve-hour weekend flights to Colorado Springs, New Orleans, and Fort Lauderdale. When some members of Congress criticized the flights to resort cities, the astronauts defended themselves by saying that they were just putting in the required flight time efficiently since they must train in other duties more than forty hours each week. Flight time in the jets costs about $2,000 per hour. The inspector general's office said that it had no evidence of "joy riding."

The Great Communicators

(Why Not the Best?)

Hey! ... I Think He's Talkin' About People from Maine!

While on the floor of the Senate discussing a $24 billion bill to aid the former Soviet states and give special status to certain immigrants, Senator Robert Byrd of West Virginia suggested that this country should no longer admit immigrants who can't speak English. "Our own people are out of work. We have homeless people in the streets. What are we doing, opening up another door here for more immigrants who can't speak English?" Byrd continued: "I pick up the telephone and call the local garage. I can't understand the person on the other side of the line. I'm not sure he can understand me. They're all over the place, and they don't speak English. Do we want more of this?" The next day he apologized, saying that he had spoken "unwisely," in "the heat of the moment."

The Hollings Experience

- Speaking to factory workers in Hartsville, South Carolina, in 1992, U.S. Senator Ernest "Fritz" Hollings suggested that they "should draw a mushroom cloud and put underneath it: 'Made in America by lazy and illiterate workers and tested in Japan.'" After being branded a "Japan basher," for the incident, Hollings said that he was responding to comments from Japanese politicians who called American workers lazy.

- In 1993, commenting on upcoming trade talks in Geneva, Hollings said, "Everybody likes to go to Geneva. I used to do it for the Law of the Sea conferences and you'd find these potentates from down in Africa, you know, rather than eating each other, they'd just come up and get a good square meal in Geneva."

- "We've got this—what is it, Buffcoat and Beaver, or Beaver and something else they had—I haven't seen it, I don't watch it, but whatever it is, it was at 7 P.M. ... [MTV] put it on now at 10:30, I think. They've pleaded guilty, and they'll do it as long as you and I have hearings."—Senator Ernest F. Hollings on *Beavis and Butt-head* during Senate hearings on violence on television.

(Personal note to the reader: I know that you must be just as delighted as I am that in these times when we [if you, like me, live in a major metropolitan area] are afraid to throw out the trash at night, our U.S. Senate can take the time to sit and worry endlessly over cartoon characters as if they were real people. Of course, if you look closely at the actual quotation above, you'll see a man talking about something, he's not sure what, because he doesn't know the title of the show, has never seen it, and "thinks" it's been moved from its time period—and all because of his mere presence in Washington. Such command of the popular culture. He's really in touch with you and me. . . . NEXT!)

How Many Times a Day Does a Member of Congress Think About Sex?

As Representative Martin Hoke (R., Ohio) and another House freshman waited to give their comments on the President's State of the Union speech in 1994, a young female producer was preparing the scene for television broadcast to their home state. After she had placed microphones on the two, she stepped behind them to check something. Unbeknownst to Hoke, the video camera was already on and running. It captured him turning around to watch the producer and commenting to his fellow member of Congress, "She has the *beeeg* breasts."

Hoke had drawn attention soon after coming to Washington. *The New York Times* quoted him as saying that he could see himself dating two newly elected congresswomen because "they're hot."

When Honesty Rears Its Head . . .

"I had the good fortune to spend the break in the Virgin Islands. I can say that now because I'm not running for re-election. I've been doing it for years, but now I can admit it."—Representative William Ford (D., Michigan), chairman of the Education and Labor Committee, speaking to his colleagues during a Rules Committee meeting.

Okay . . .

"Please listen to me, because I don't want anyone to think that what we're doing is what we're doing."—Representative Bill Thomas of California, trying to explain why he and other Republican members were calling up the President's health reform plan for a vote in his subcommittee.

Now That You Ask

"What are you doing here, jackin' me around with these other politicians that are so dumb?"—Representative James Traficant (D., Ohio) to ABC-TV reporter John Stossel. Stossel had just asked whether the tributes Traficant makes to individuals on the House floor, which thus become part of the *Congressional Record*, aren't really just a waste of taxpayer money.

Being a Member of Congress Means Never Having to Say You're Sorry

During a speech to a Human Rights Campaign Fund meeting in 1994 Representative Steve C. Gunderson (R., Wisconsin) "appear[ed] comfortable at least leaving the impression that he is gay," wrote *The Milwaukee Journal*. Days later on the floor of the House Representative Bob Dornan (R., California), in the middle of a debate, spoke to Gunderson directly: "He's in, he's out, he's in, he's out, he's in. I guess you're out because you went up and spoke to a large homosexual dinner, Mr. Gunderson." If you were lucky enough to be watching C-SPAN at the time, you could have heard this yourself. You'll never read it in the *Congressional Record*, though, because Dornan had his remarks stricken (taking advantage of the right of each member to make any remark, no matter how stupid or meanspirited and have it not exist in the formal record). However, speaking to a *States News* reporter outside the House chamber afterward, Dornan called Gunderson a "homo."

And Probably Members of Congress, Too

When Representative Edward Roybal visited the new Edward R. Roybal Center and Federal Building (what a coincidence, it's named after him) in Los Angeles, his eyes fell upon a sculpture in the courtyard of a nude woman holding an equally nude infant. After Roybal noticed two young boys touching the sculpted infant's genitals, he said that the work should be removed because it would "attract the homeless . . . perverts [and] graffiti artists."

Well, He Was Right in His Preface

Frederick K. Goodwin, administrator of the Health and Human Services Department's Alcohol, Drug Abuse, and Mental Health Administration during the Bush administration, was discussing urban violence at a public meeting when he drew an analogy between studies of aggressive male monkeys in the jungle and violent inner-city youth. After speaking of a jungle scene in which "roughly half of [male monkeys] survive to adulthood" and the "other half die by violence," Goodwin said that "high impact inner-city areas" have lost "some of the civilizing evolutionary things that we have built up." Before embarking on his comparisons, Goodwin said, "I say this with the realization that it might be easily misunderstood."

Government by Lovable Old Coots, for Lovable Old Coots

Back in 1990 Veterans Affairs Secretary Edward Derwinski said that it was "just one of those dumb slips . . . that law of averages you have them, I guess." He was explaining his use of the term "wetbacks" to refer to illegal Hispanic immigrants. He said it while out on the campaign trail on behalf of a Republican congressional candidate in Omaha. Asked at a breakfast meeting what his department was doing to fight the drug problem, Derwinski commented that the drug cartel "even uses wetbacks to get drugs into the country."

- Derwinski earlier came under criticism when it was revealed that he had nicknames for each of his personal staff at the department. The names for female staffers included Little Miss Coffee Maker, Little Miss Muffet, Zsa Zsa, and Miss America. He usually referred to women he didn't know as "angel." Said Derwinski: "All my life I've given people nicknames and pet names. . . . It's just one of my idiosyncratic ways."

How Many Parties Can One Offensive Joke Offend?

Speaking before an international audience at the 1989 Pacific Summit Trade Conference in Seattle, Fred M. Zeder II, then head of the United States Overseas Private Investment Corporation, started his remarks with a joke in which former Chinese Chairman Mao Zedong is asked by a reporter what "might have happened if Lee Harvey Oswald had assassinated Khrushchev rather than President Kennedy." In a mock Chinese accent, Zeder had Mao respond: "Only one thing certain. Aristotle Onassis would not have married Mrs. Khrushchev." Said a Chinese diplomat in attendance: "I don't like the joke. He's a joker. I don't know what his purpose was."

See: Hollings, Fritz

Speaking at a breakfast meeting with reporters in 1992, Treasury Secretary Nicholas F. Brady said, "We have been told our workers are idle and ill educated, our goods uncompetitive, and our managers inefficient, and we can't compete with the Japs or the Germans or for that matter anybody else in the world."

How Does That Selection Process Go Again?

While awaiting congressional confirmation for his nomination to head the Office of Juvenile Justice and Delinquency Prevention in the Reagan administration, Alfred Regnery was asked by reporters why his family station wagon sported the bumper sticker "Have You Slugged Your Kid Today?" Regnery explained, "You've seen the ones that say, 'Have You Hugged Your Kid Today?' Well, this is a takeoff."

In Case You Missed It

Back in 1990 the Strategic Air Command, headquartered in Omaha, Nebraska, changed its thirty-two-year-old motto, "Peace is our profession." The replacement motto is "War is our profession—peace is our product." The change was made at the behest of the SAC commander, General John T. Chain, Jr., who found the latter to be more accurate according to his view.

Who Wants to Know?

Testifying before the House Banking Committee in 1990, Federal Reserve Chairman Alan Greenspan was asked whether the Fed would cut interest rates. Said Greenspan: "I can give you a qualified answer, but it would be so muddled it wouldn't be useful to you."

What to Say When Totally Surprised

Commenting on an accord reached between Germany's Helmut Kohl and Soviet leader Mikhail Gorbachev, Secretary of State James Baker said, "This is a delightful surprise to the extent that it is a surprise, and it is only a surprise to the extent that we anticipated."

Sorry for the Apologies

The latest in a line of U.S. government apologies came in November 1993. The U.S. Senate voted 65 to 34 to apologize formally to Hawaii for the fact that the United States overthrew Queen Liliuokalani in 1893. The resolution "apologizes to Native Hawaiians on behalf of the people of the United States for the overthrow of the Kingdom of Hawaii on Jan. 17, 1893, with the participation of agents and citizens of the United States, and the deprivation of the rights of native Hawaiians to self-determination." The formal apology also urged that steps be taken "to provide a proper foundation for reconciliation between the United States and the native Hawaiian people." Reportedly many of the thirty-four voting against were just sick of making apologies.

In a Class (and a World) of His Own

- Former Vice President Dan Quayle on the old proverb "Give a man a fish and you feed him for a day. Teach a man to fish and you feed him for a lifetime": "If you give a person a fish, they'll fish for a day. But if you train a person to fish, they'll fish for a lifetime."
- On why the United States should explore Mars: "Mars is essentially in the same orbit. Mars is somewhat the same distance from the sun, which is very important. We have seen pictures where there are

canals, we believe, and water. If there is water, there is oxygen. If oxygen, that means we can breathe."

- Replying to a question about Hawaii's universal health care model: "Hawaii is a unique state. It is a small state. It is a state that is by itself. It is a—it is different than the other forty-nine states. Well, all states are different, but it's got a particularly unique situation."

Got It!

According to a memo from the Office of Management and Budget in the early 1980s, "An agency subject to the provisions of the Federal Reports Act may enter into an arrangement with an organization not subject to the Act whereby the organization not subject to the Act collects information on behalf of the agency subject to the Act. The reverse also occurs."

Am I Locked or Loaded or Both?

Marine Corps Commandant Alfred M. Gray, testifying before Congress in 1989 on the military's role in fighting the war on drugs: "And as we look at both the demand and the supply side challenges—and they are immense—in terms of the money involved, in terms of the complexity, in terms of the impact, I think that initiatives are bubbling up, initiatives are being looked at, people are fully locked and loaded to be pro-active here—and already pro-active."

Used-Car Dealers, All

Professor William Lutz, author of the book *Doublespeak*, suggests that Washington's mangling of language "is not a slip of the tongue, or language used out of ignorance, but is instead a very conscious use of language as a weapon or tool by those in power to achieve their ends at our expense." He explains the search during the Reagan administration for the right words to discuss a tax increase. Officials moved from "tax enhancement" to "revenue enhancement" to "tax base broadening" to "tax base erosion control" to, finally, "update the revenue mechanism." (Much like the use by the Clinton administration of the term "investment" when speaking of spending federal dollars.)

- Richard Mitchell, editor of the *Underground Grammarian* newsletter, also tracks Washington-speak. Says Mitchell: "Nobody in Washington can speak clearly. This is not a flaw in grammar. This is a flaw in character." During the Iran-contra hearings back in 1987 Mitchell noted that witnesses regularly twisted the language. Two made up new verbs such as "Chinese-wall" ("It's traditional for the FBI to ... Chinese-wall itself from the Justice Department") and "fly-speck" (he "did not fly-speck" the CIA's role). Retired Major General Richard Secord spoke of "lethal assistance" when he was talking about weapons, and former Ambassador Lewis Tambs remarked that retired General John Singlaub referred to U.S. citizens as "United Statesians."

Whew! I Feel Better Now

Senator Ernest Hollings, criticizing the Senate for not addressing the difficult issues of the day: "Congress is not corrupt. Congress is not on the take. Congress is incompetent."

Rules and Regulations

Games People Play

In 1990 *The Fort Worth Star-Telegram* reported that a Housing and Urban Development program designed to help the homeless was really benefiting some very wealthy people. Under the federal homeless housing guidelines, 10 percent of fifty thousand foreclosed homes owned by the government nationwide are made available to HUD-approved sponsors, who then lease the homes for one year to those qualifying for assistance. The sponsors can have two-year options to buy the homes at prices 10 percent below the market value and can in turn sell the homes at market rates. The cases investigated by the newspaper found wealthy HUD sponsors who were leasing the homes for themselves. When one small church near Keller, Texas, became a HUD sponsor, its members leased ninety-seven government homes and placed friends and families in them. The newspaper also found evidence of four Fort Worth area church pastors or their family members living in the homes, along with several businessmen also participating, one the owner of a million-dollar company. HUD regulations (as of 1990) defined a homeless person as anyone without a permanent home, regardless of his or her income.

1834. 1994. Hmm ...

According to the Trading with Indians Act of 1834, many employees of the federal Indian Health Service or the Bureau of Indian Affairs are in violation of the law because they are married to American Indians who work on reservations and own businesses. The law prohibits "commercial" trading with American Indians by any IHS or BIA employee or "in the name of a family member or spouse" of such employee. As the federal government (which, along with the tribal government, is the biggest employer on most reservations) has hired more Native Americans with spouses who live on the reservations, violations of the act have grown. Many of those employees have received letters warning them that their situation would be "cause for severe disciplinary action, as well as criminal penalties." According to reporter Jack Anderson, because of the law, IHS employees are prevented from even selling Avon products in neighborhoods with predominantly Native American populations. "This is one of those anachronisms," said Representative Jon Kyl (R., Arizona). "The law was needed back one hundred and fifty years ago, but now you don't need it. This is just one of those things we ought to get off the books because unfortunately real people are in violation of real law and we don't intend for that situation to exist."

Think Before You Swat

With the placement of the Delhi sands fly on the federal endangered species list, the mayor of Colton, California, feared for the future of a 300-acre enterprise zone. That's because 3 acres of the fly's habitat are inside the enterprise zone. Of the habitat's original 25,600 acres, only 512 remain. While no one knows how many of the flies are in existence, there were sightings in the summer and fall of 1993. Environmentalists and agriculture officials warn that the fly is a part of an ecosystem, and its extinction could lead to the death of other parts of the system. Said the mayor of Colton: "They talk about the fly becoming extinct, but so are jobs. Next are we going to be designating ants?" While no building plans were derailed, the mayor noted that the announcement about the fly forced some developers to have second thoughts. According to the rules of the endangered species list, anyone killing or harming one of the flies is subject to a $200,000 fine and a year in jail.

Just What Was the Intent of That Rule?

Rules protecting the red-cockaded woodpecker put parts of North Carolina timber farmer Ben Cone's land off-limits to forestry uses. Cone said that $1.8 million in timber was caught in the protected zone. His response? Cone clear-cut all other trees on his land in an effort to prevent the woodpeckers from spreading to any more of his trees and thus putting any more of his property under the protective rules.

Where's the Pamphlet *How to Take Advantage of Cheap Foreign Labor?*

The "Basic Pamphlets List," a product of the U.S. Information Agency's Special Publications Branch, is a catalog of United States publications that are available only to this country's diplomats. The list offers everything from portraits of the President to pamphlets entitled *Democracy and Defense: Civilian Control of the Military in the United States* and *Golden Door: U.S. Immigration and Ellis Island.* All publications are designed to be stocked at or distributed by U.S. embassies and are unavailable to you and me. "Anything that offers even a hint of propagandizing the American people is forbidden," said Howard Cincotta, the preparer of the list. Besides being informative, the pamphlets are very cheap. This is because they are printed in Manila. Cincotta said that previous printing plants, in Beirut and Mexico, were lost to war and earthquake respectively.

Catch-22 No. 5,242

Federal law enforcement officers fighting the growth of "crank" or "speed" labs in California are being hampered by environmental consequences of the busts. With every illegal lab that is closed, Department of Justice lab specialists are stuck with the task of disposing of large quantities of benzene (a carcinogen), ether, acids, and other dangerous chemicals. The department allocates $700,000 annually for cleaning up the toxics, but each lab bust results in disposal costs of $7,000 to $10,000. The department has been forced to apply other budget funds to cover the growing price tag.

To Every Season, Turn, Turn, Turn, There Are Comments on a Proposed Rule Change, Turn, Turn, Turn

A group of U.S. senators asked the chairman of the Nuclear Regulatory Commission to bypass agency regulations to order immediately that nuclear power plants be protected by barriers from potential car bomb attacks. After the World Trade Center bombing the senators looked into nuclear plant protection and found that the regulations mandate that complexes need be protected only against terrorists on foot and make no provision for terrorists in vehicles. An advisory committee to the NRC said that proposed safety changes needed to be analyzed by the "probabilistic risk assessment" system which is to be used when considering any plant improvement. An NRC spokesman also noted that the staff is analyzing comments on the proposed rule change. The senators asked that all this be avoided and car barriers be erected now. "Undertaking a probabilistic risk assessment at this point would turn a matter of common sense into a complicated mathematical exercise," they charged.

Only One-Armed Dutch Ballerinas Named Sam Need Apply

The Labor Department's H2B visa program, begun in 1986, allows businesses in the United States to import temporary foreign workers if domestic ones can't be found. About two thirds of three thousand annual requests for such temp help are approved. The requirements of the program are that employers explain the shortage and advertise for at least three days for domestic help. According to the approved applicants, in 1992 there was a shortage of fish egg attendants, palm readers, coaches, singers, circus aerialists, seafood processors, ride supervisors, and travel guides. That same year the program admitted seven bakers, twenty-six chefs, two pastry chefs, and three sous-chefs. A report on the program in the *Wall Street Journal* found that while some abused the program by specifically listing job requirements pertinent only to an already selected foreigner, other jobs had to be filled by foreigners because Americans clearly didn't want them. In the former category, a boxing promoter who wanted to import two specific Canadian boxers for a match had the ad looking for American boxers placed in *The New York Times* want ads. The latter category included people to help skiers off ski lift chairs for $5.50 per hour and jobs detonating avalanche-prone areas with dynamite at $7.30 per hour.

The Maltese Heron

When Carol Bentz of Manchester, Maryland, wanted to have her dying pet, a blue heron named Steve, stuffed and donated to a high school, she discovered that transporting a dead heron, which is a protected bird, is punishable by a federal fine of up to $5,000 and six months in jail and a state fine of $1,000 and one year in jail. While looking for someone with a permit to transport a dead heron, she also discovered that a special government permit was needed to "salvage" a dead heron. And once the dead heron is "salvaged," a private citizen is not allowed to possess the stuffed heron. When Bentz finally located a law enforcement agent of the U.S. Fish and Wildlife Service, he told her that she should freeze the bird while he started the paperwork moving on her permits. Once he discovered the location of the high school the dead bird would be donated to, that meant more permits. Finally the bird was moved and prepared by a taxidermist specially licensed for preparing protected birds. Said Bentz of the ordeal: "The government made me angry. I thought it was the stupidest thing I'd ever heard in my life."

The Final Answer to All Those Lightbulb Jokes

According to the U.S. Department of Energy, the number of workers required to accomplish the changing of one lightbulb on a safety system at its Rocky Flats, Colorado, nuclear weapons compound is forty-three. Time required: 1,087.1 worker hours.

- Responding to a congressional inquiry about how long it takes to change a lightbulb at its Oak Ridge National Laboratory in Tennessee, the department said that it takes only ninety minutes at a cost of $136. How is that billed to the government? Well, thirty minutes were taken up waiting for someone to arrive to open the building where the bulb needed to be changed. Putting on protective clothing (the bulb was in a radiation danger area), changing the bulb, and taking off the clothing amounted to ten minutes. The remaining fifty minutes were for the time it took for the bulb changer to get to the building and return to his office. Simple.

Why They Call Them Bureaucrats

Among about two billion other things, the *Federal Personnel Manual* gives federal supervisors explicit instructions on how to put a name on a file folder. According to the rules, the name should appear: "LAST NAME (comma) SUFFIX (Jr., Sr., etc.) (comma) (space) FIRST NAME or INITIAL (space) MIDDLE NAME(s) or INITIAL(s)." In that wild scenario where the subject may not have a middle name or initial, one is instructed to "enter NMN." Glad we got that straight. The manual consists of three volumes, each as large as the telephone book of a major city, and thirty supplemental volumes. There are also nine volumes of bulletins listing all changes since the manual was last printed. Several hundred pages of the manual are devoted solely to the task of dismissing employees who have performed unsatisfactorily. (Four months after the Clinton administration suggested eliminating the manual, the Office of Personnel Management eliminated more than 86 percent of its rules and regulations. By the end of 1994 the manual was to be replaced by a much-streamlined document.)

Why They Have Those Hundreds of Pages on How to Fire an Employee

After employees of the federal Bonneville Power Administration in Portland, Oregon, complained of wet typewriter keys, yellow-stained sweaters, and office plants that were dying, an infrared camera was installed in their work area. It soon captured a computer specialist in the office urinating on various things. His superiors put him on administrative leave (which gave him a full paycheck) and entered him into a treatment program. After six months it was determined that he shouldn't be returned to his workplace, and termination was recommended. Nine months later, months in which he continued to receive his paycheck, he was discharged. The employee immediately appealed his termination to the Merit Systems Protection Board and six months later won the appeal. The judge ruled that the employee posed no threat to fellow workers and ordered him reinstated at his old job and reimbursed for lost back pay. At last report, the BPA appealed the ruling, but the man was back on the payroll and still not in the workplace.

Hey! Now That You Broke Them All, We've Got to Reorder Five Hundred Thousand of Them (We Can Put Them in All Government Offices Where Smoking Is Forbidden Anyway)

One of the big targets of Vice President Al Gore's reinventing government initiative was the federal procurement system. As he noted, government regulations on the purchase of an ashtray ran for nine pages. The specifications listed "the precise dimensions, color, polish and markings required." One requirement was that when an ashtray is broken, it shatter into no more than thirty-five pieces. This was ensured by smashing sample ashtrays under consideration and counting the shards of glass.

Why You Should No Longer Fight for Your Right to Party When in a National Forest

In early 1994 the U.S. Department of Agriculture published rules in the *Federal Register* making it a class B misdemeanor to "cuss, scream or play the radio loudly" in a national forest. Said a spokesperson for the Forest Service: "If you've got a naughty person whose unlicensed dog is off the leash, chasing wildlife, they've chopped a hole in the picnic table, they're drunk and noisy, they're using signs for firewood and they refer to you and your mother in derogatory terms, well, they'll probably get a ticket."

Next Time You See a Mushroom Cloud, You'll Know That the Best Interests of the Environment Were Foremost in Their Minds

In the interests of protecting the ozone layer, the U.S. Air Force is planning to retrofit all its nuclear missiles with cooling systems that do not use chlorofluorocarbons (CFCs). An Air Force spokeswoman said that the action is "part of pollution prevention. We have a program to eliminate ozone-depleting chemicals." The retrofit program is in response to an Environmental Protection Agency proposal to ban all production and imports of CFCs by January 1, 1996. Said an EPA spokesperson: "I can see how it may seem a little . . . ironic. The depletion of the ozone presents a real danger to the whole world. We're not going to make exceptions to the rules for something like this."

Things Like This Always Make Sense in Washington

During the summer of 1993 former Acting Army Secretary John Shannon was put on administrative leave after he was caught shoplifting $30 worth of women's clothing from an Army exchange. He confessed to the crime and was put in a counseling program for shoplifting. A few months later the Pentagon hired him as an

$85,000-a-year consultant. Among his responsibilities as a consultant was advising the Pentagon's Inventory Review Task Force: reviewing Pentagon inventories and deciding what to keep and what to get rid of. (Within about one month of the announcement about his being rehired, Shannon left his consultancy, reportedly because of pressure from outraged Pentagon officials.)

Wait, I've Got It! A Really, Really Big Moat!

Since 1989 the Rocky Flats weapons plant in Colorado has sat dormant. The plant produced plutonium triggers for nuclear weapons, but production was stopped that year because of safety concerns. With the Department of Energy now faced with the problem of how to clean up the site, the plant manager suggests that it should be buried. Mark Silverman, calling his plan a "monument to the Cold War," said that the 14.2 tons of plutonium now sitting in seven buildings in the complex be moved and consolidated in just one. Then the buildings could be buried. "For the foreseeable future, which is in excess of twenty-four thousand years, people aren't going to use this land," Silverman said.

And While We're on the Subject ...

For more than ten years now the federal government has been paying consultants to try to come up with a way to warn people thousands of years in the future to stay away from nuclear dump sites. One consultant, Thomas A. Sebeok, a professor of linguistics and anthropology, suggested back in 1984 the development of "curse of the Pharaoh" type of myths to scare people from the sites. In his scenario, delivered to the Department of Energy's Office of Nuclear Waste Isolation in a thirty-three-page report, Sebeok suggested that the myths be kept alive by an "atomic priesthood" created by the Department of Energy. The "priesthood," consisting of scientists and scholars, would be self-perpetuating. "When one member dies, the others would choose to initiate a replacement." The professor, who claims to have been inspired by watching old "monster movies," said that the myths should be used only in conjunction with more standard efforts, such as fences and gates.

- A more recent DOE study by Sandia National Laboratories titled "Expert Judgment on Markers to Deter Inadvertent Human Intrusion into the Waste Isolation Pilot Plant" considered protective systems for a potential nuclear waste storage site. This study included the use of ancient facial masks designed to induce dread and more modern facial icons showing such emotions as fright and panic. However, experts are concerned about what unimagined future events could mean to the security of the sites. As one DOE consultant said in 1994, "Human beings have gotten pretty good at looking into deep space, but we are really no good at looking into deep time."

Beagle Dog Attack Squadron on Standby Alert

The Interior Department is spending $100,000 to train beagles to sniff out brown tree snakes in Hawaii. The tree snakes are not in Hawaii in any noticeable number as of yet. However, they are on Guam. Since being introduced onto that island, they have destroyed a large number of bird species and developed a habit of crawling onto electrical transformers (causing seventy-four power outages in 1990 alone). The density of brown snakes on Guam is now estimated at fifteen thousand per square mile. Don't panic! The beagles will stand ready until needed.

Hey, I Hear They're Handing Out Matches to Go with the Free Dynamite!

According to a report by the General Accounting Office and the minority staff of the Senate Committee on Aging, Social Security programs dispensed $1.4 billion in cash during 1993 to more than 250,000 alcoholics and drug addicts, who, instead of using it for recovery purposes, were feeding their habits. "Hundreds of millions of scarce federal dollars are flowing directly to drug addicts, who are turning around and buying heroin, cocaine, and other illegal drugs on the street the very same day," said Senator William S. Cohen (R., Maine). The report found that only 78,000 of the beneficiaries were subject to any monitoring of the money they received. In some cases persons appointed to handle the funds for addicts were themselves addicted to drugs or alcohol. One liquor store owner in Denver was found to have received $160,000 a year from the program on behalf of 40 alcoholics whom he kept supplied with alcohol. Cohen suggested switching from cash disbursements to food vouchers or direct payments to recovery facilities. (Within days the Senate had passed an amendment proposed by Cohen designed to prevent drug dealers from receiving federal disability payments. The current law demands that individuals show that they are unable to perform gainful employment. The amendment would consider illegal income, such as that from drug dealing, gainful activity, thus making a person engaged in such activity ineligible for benefits. I get it. So when you ask them if they've got a job and they say, "Yeah, I sell drugs," the clerk will know to stop processing that application. Whew! Pretty clever.)

The Never-Ending Reagan Revolution

Over the last three years Congress has authorized more than $65 million in funds for the CIA to use to buy back what remains of the estimated 1,000 Stinger missiles that it distributed to the Afghan rebels in their fight against the Soviets in the 1980s. The agency and others fear that the thirty-five-pound missile, designed to bring down an aircraft, will be sold to terrorists on the black market. Some intelligence officials estimate that about 350 were fired during the war, and as many as 400 unused ones remain in the hands of the mujahideein. Some of the missiles have already surfaced in Iran, Qatar, and North Korea. The original cost of each missile was $35,000 when the U.S. Army bought it from General Dynamics. In 1990 the CIA was offering $50,000 per missile in the buy-back program. Now the price has reportedly risen to $100,000 per Stinger. One of the Afghan tribal leaders, Abdul Salam, is known by the popular name "Rocketi" because of the vast number of surface-to-air missiles he acquired from many foreign sources during the war.

The U.S. Postal Service

(Or, Why I'll Never See My Mail Ever Again)

Makes Sense to Me, Beavis

Following a year of $500 million in losses and the start of a new year that found the U.S. Postal Service running expenses of $215 million more than expected, the postmaster general, Marvin Runyon, announced the possibility of large cash bonuses for his top managers if the total loss for the current year could be kept to only $1.3 billion. Under the terms of the incentive program the nearly one thousand eligible executives could qualify for bonuses of up to 10 percent of their annual salaries if the Postal Service meets three criteria: achieving its financial goal, satisfying customers, and keeping employees happy. With postal executives earning average annual salaries of $83,000, all the executives could share in a $9 million bonus pool. (Within weeks the Postal Service proposed raising the price of a first-class stamp to 32 cents from 29 cents effective in early 1995.)

(Note to the reader: Throughout this section it might

be helpful to keep repeating to yourself: "The U.S. Postal Service lost five hundred million dollars in 1993, but it wants to pay bonuses for losing only one-point-three billion dollars." Just a suggestion.)

It Is How You Look That Counts

Despite having to terminate 30,000 employees in a streamlining effort and losing $500 million in fiscal 1993, the U.S. Postal Service spent $7 million to replace its corporate logo. The new logo, sporting an eagle's head flying into the wind, was designed by CYB Yasumura Design Inc. for $100,000. In a letter to 680,000 postal employees, Postmaster General Marvin Runyon called the new logo "a clean break with our bureaucratic past." The logo will be phased into all markets at a cost of about $1 million per year over the next six years. The agency will spend $600,000 in announcing the change to employees and suppliers. (Runyon, who refers to the new logo as the sonic eagle, was also responsible for the redesign of the Tennessee Valley Authority's logo while he headed that agency from 1988 to 1992.) In a letter to postal facilities, the service's corporate relations office warned employees to use the new logo properly, specifying the proper color backgrounds on which to print it and insisting that the "eagle's head within the box must remain white." The letter called the new logo the "cornerstone of the USPS communications message."

If This Is the Postal Service's Idea of a Good Deal, I'm Beginning to Understand About That $500 Million Loss

(*Background:* While the Postal Service has a monopoly on all first-class letters, in 1979 an exemption was created for letters that needed to be at a destination by noon the next day. With the creation of Federal Express and other overnight services, postal inspectors are always on the lookout for violations: non-time-sensitive materials being shipped by the other services.)

Early in 1994 a postal inspector audit announced that five federal agencies (the Government Services Administration and the departments of Health and Human Services, Treasury, Energy, and Agriculture) were violating the Postal Service's monopoly by using Federal Express for first-class mail shipments. The audit said that the five agencies accounted for one third of the 4.3 million government packages sent by Federal Express in two years. (No wonder government mailroom personnel are turning to Federal Express: It's cheaper! In 1991 the GSA contracted with Federal Express for next-day deliveries at a price of $3.75. The Postal Service's Express Mail service was the standard $9.95 per package!)

Throwing Stones

Representative Mac Collins (R., Georgia) criticized the Postal Service for delivering its 1993 annual report to his congressional office by private courier. In a letter to Postmaster General Marvin Runyon, Collins called the move a "blatant example of waste and mismanagement." A USPS spokesperson said that Collins and some other members of Congress received their reports by courier because of mistakes in the addresses!

Limbo of the Lost

For some unknown reason a number of Christmas cards mailed by the office of Vice President Al Gore in early December 1993 didn't reach their destinations in Tennessee until ten weeks later. The delayed deliveries came to light the same week that Gore's task force on government reform praised the USPS for improved customer service. Said a USPS spokesperson: "The bottom line is that we're real embarrassed. This is an anomaly." (In December 1992 the USPS lost a container of holiday mail at an Arkansas airport. That batch of mail contained numerous invitations from President-elect Clinton inviting friends to his inauguration ceremonies.)

- In the summer of 1991 attorneys defending the Postal Service in an employment discrimination suit filed their expert witness list with the court via the service's Express Mail. The list had to be at the court in Dayton, Ohio, on August 1. The attorneys mailed the list from Philadelphia, using the overnight service on July 30, with the guarantee that it would be delivered by noon the next day. The witness list didn't arrive until ten days later. This forced the lawyer representing the Postal Service to file a motion asking the court to allow late submission of the list because of slow mail delivery.

- In mid-1988 Texas officials were unable to carry out the execution of convicted murderer Ramon Montoya because his death warrant failed to arrive before his scheduled execution date. The warrant was mailed more than one month before the date on which Montoya was to die. Officials rescheduled the execution for December 1, 1988, before the bulk of the Christmas mailing rush.

Why These People Are So Tense

Left-handed postal workers can thank Robert Green, an employee of the Seattle Post Office, for winning the right to sort mail with either hand. Green was the first left-hander to fight and win against postal manual regulations which said that mail had to be sorted with the right hand. "I thought it was asinine," said left-hander Green. He won, and the manual was amended.

- Postal clerk Robert McLaughlin was suspended for one week and docked $400 in wages for being "uncooperative" at a Des Moines, Iowa, training session for eight hundred postal clerks held in the early 1980s. According to McLaughlin, the goal of the seminar was to teach all clerks to "hold letters at a forty-five-degree angle and sit on a stool." He claimed to be able to sort mail just as quickly by holding it at a ninety-degree angle.

"Okay, Okay, a Mug, Twenty-nine Cents, and We Guarantee Not to Lose Your Mail for One Year!"

The Postal Service halted production of its "Legends of the West" stamp series in the middle of the press run after determining that the stamp bearing a portrait of the famous black cowboy and rodeo star Bill Pickett was actually a portrait of Pickett's brother Ben. A month after the stamp was unveiled, Pickett's descendants, led by Frank S. Phillips of Silver Spring, Maryland, went to postal authorities to tell them that they had made a mistake, which the family wanted corrected. "This is a terrible thing," said Phillips of the failed attempt to honor his great-grandfather. It was the first time in 147 years that the USPS ever released a stamp that depicted the wrong person. Although the stamps were not to be issued until March 29, 1994, many had already been distributed to post offices. Their recall was expected to cost about $1.1 million. A problem surfaced when after the recall announcement it was learned that several post offices had jumped the official sale date and sold 183 sheets for $5.80 each. These sheets, now some of the most valuable U.S. stamps in existence, have sold for as much as $12,500. But in at least one early case the post office tried to entice one of the lucky stamp owners into turning over his copy by offering him twenty-nine cents and an official U.S. Postal Service coffee mug. He reportedly didn't go for it.

Either Rain, Snow, or Gloom of Night Will Now Delay the U.S. Mail

The Postal Service blamed a drop in mail delivery during the winter of 1994 on three months of ice and snow-storms that plagued the East Coast. In the first three months of 1994 the percentage of letters delivered over-night declined to 79 percent from 83 percent a year earlier. The volume of letters scheduled to be delivered in two days dropped to 67 percent from 75 percent, and three-day deliveries fell to 65 percent from 77 percent. The service said that the weather crippled all forms of transportation, closing airports and highways essential to deliver the mail.

How About That New Slogan, "It'll Get There When It Gets There"?

On March 24, 1994, Postmaster General Marvin Runyon ordered that the service no longer advertise or claim that its Priority Mail service can guarantee "two-day" mail service because too much of the "two-day" mail cannot be delivered within the time guarantee. Runyon also ordered that all envelopes bearing the "two-day" claim be destroyed. That will cost at least $185,000. Sen-ator David Pryor (D., Arkansas), head of the Senate Governmental Affairs Federal Services, Post Office, and Civil Service Subcommittee, said in 1993 that only 77 percent of the USPS Priority Mail letters were actually being delivered within the promised time frame. Runyon said that in 1994 that figure had risen to 84 percent.

He Seemed So Quiet

Speaking at a forum sponsored by the Postal Service, Dennis L. Johnson, president of Behavior Analysts and Consultants, released his company's portrait of the typical workplace killer. On the basis of studying 125 homicide cases between 1984 and 1993, Johnson said that the killer is a male loner frustrated with problems at work and having few relationships outside the workplace. Johnson said that the average age of the workplace killer is thirty-six and that he used guns in 81 percent of the recorded cases. The killer committed suicide in one quarter of the incidents. Johnson noted a modern tendency for people to blame others for their problems, thus creating in their minds an injustice being done to them when a supervisor criticizes them or dismisses them. Speaking at the same meeting was Postmaster General Marvin Runyon. He noted that murder had become the third-ranked cause of death on the job in this country and the number one cause for women.

- Postal union officials (four unions regulate every aspect of a postal worker's day) claim that although the service will have spent $4 billion on automation by 1995, the streamlined processing of the mail has actually added to worker stress, not reduced it as intended. Each hour of a postal clerk's day is divided into a hundred parts. Some supervisors keep tabs on employee performance against that hundred-part-per-hour schedule.

Hey, Moe! Hey, Larry!

A 1992 investigation into drug dealing at the Cleveland Post Office by the U.S. Postal Inspection Service resulted in the arrest of nineteen postal workers and a community activist. All stood accused of dealing. However, when the first case went to trial, a judge determined that the man speaking on a tape of an alleged drug deal was not the defendant in his courtroom. A subsequent investigation determined that the postal inspection agency had been taken by a group of six supposed informers. The six took more than $250,000 in postal funds that they were supposed to use in setting up drug transactions. Instead they pocketed the money, made bogus tape recordings of phony drug deals, and set up nineteen innocent men for arrest. Tests found that the drugs the six supposedly purchased consisted of a little cocaine mixed with a lot of baking soda. Representative Bill Clay (D., Missouri), chairman of the House Post Office and Civil Service Committee, sharply criticized the service for the botched investigation. He noted that several of the nineteen innocent men lost their reputations, marriages, and homes, and one attempted suicide. Clay's committee also found that the Postal Service rehired the nineteen only after "the intervention of the committee" and that promised payments of back pay were slow in coming. "What is purported to be a top-flight, professional law enforcement organization is revealed as a gang of undisciplined yahoos, out of control," said Clay.

"Hey, Wait a Minute, Mr. Postman!"

When a Greeley, Colorado, mail carrier moved out of his house, the new residents found that he had left behind eight thousand pieces of undelivered mail. While much of the stash consisted of bulk mail, it also included pieces such as a $2,900 tax refund check. A postal inspector investigating the case explained that the carrier sometimes didn't finish his daily route and brought the mail home instead of returning it to the office. As the stash grew, so did his fear of returning it. Postmark dates on the undelivered mail ranged from April 1, 1991, to February 24, 1992. If convicted, he faces up to five years in prison. The postman's career with the service lasted more than thirteen years.

- Three years earlier postal inspectors in Boulder, Colorado, located another stash of mail from a postal carrier's backyard. Investigators needed wheelbarrows to remove three and a quarter tons of undelivered mail and a half ton of postal equipment from the fifteen-year veteran's property. Officials were alerted by complaints from his neighbors that bags of paper and bulk mail were piling up in his yard.
- A substitute postal carrier in Iowa refused to deliver issues of *Time* and *Newsweek* magazines because their covers would have tempted people to sin, he said. The cover of *Newsweek* in question pictured two lesbian women hugging under the title "Lesbi-

ans Coming Out Strong: What Are the Limits of Tolerance?" The *Time* cover showed a prostitute dressed in a bikini on a bar patron's lap. Carrier George Yoerger left the magazines behind at the post office when he went out on his route. Told by a supervisor that he had to deliver the magazines or quit his job, Yoerger quit. "As a follower of Jesus Christ, the only choice open to me was the latter," he said.

• In January 1994 Postal Service inspectors sent test letters to Chicago post offices in order to observe the delivery system there. The letters turned up in a Minneapolis dead-letter office. In February 1994 postal inspectors in Chicago found forty thousand pieces of two-month-old undelivered mail in a letter carrier's delivery truck. The carrier was suspended. The following month in Chicago an undelivered two-hundred-pound stack of mail was found burning on a footpath under a viaduct. A letter carrier was charged with the dumping. Within hours investigators found twenty thousand pieces of undelivered mail dating back to the 1970s packed into trash cans in the basement of a former carrier's house two miles away from the burn site. The retired carrier admitted to hiding that mail because he couldn't deliver it on time. Postal officials said that all the Chicago area finds were unrelated to one another. In the latter two cases the bulk of the mail consisted of junk mail. (During the 1993 fiscal year, about one third of Chicago's residents complained of poor mail service.) When Postmaster General Marvin Runyon rushed to Chicago to conduct a forum with city residents, he was awash in horror stories. One resident hadn't received any mail since the previous July. One woman's phone bill, mailed in November, turned up in Australia in January.

- In April 1994, again in Chicago, postal inspectors located five thousand pieces of undelivered mail, some as old as seven years, two thousand pieces of it stashed behind the home of one carrier and three thousand pieces in the trunk of another carrier's car. At least one federal income tax return was found in the pile. (These incidents brought the total amount of undelivered mail located in Chicago in the first four months of 1993 to seventy thousand pieces.)
- In May 1994 firefighters responding to a fire at a Chicago condominium discovered twenty-three hundred pounds of letters, packages, and advertising circulars at the home of another letter carrier. The mail, some dating to 1988, included more than twenty-five hundred first-class letters and three hundred parcels.
- To add insult to injury, it was also revealed that the manager of the Chicago mail plant spent $200,000 to have a bathroom and kitchen added to her office despite the fact that the operation would soon be relocated at a new facility a block away. A postal spokesperson said that the manager "didn't use very good judgment." When officials realized what the scope of the office renovation was, they ordered the manager not to use it and instead turned it into a conference room.

Yeah! More Vodka
Presents All Around!

In San Fernando, California, postal carrier Floyd Sterling, thirty-four, pleaded no contest to charges that he shot and killed a family's dog while delivering their mail. Sterling shot Skippy, the German shepherd, the day after Christmas 1989. His reason for the shooting was that the dog had bitten him earlier in the year and was again threatening him. Skippy's owner, Tammy Brody, said that Sterling "freaked out" and shot her dog just as she was emerging from her house with a bottle of vodka she intended to give the carrier as a Christmas present. Neighbors along the route said that the dog was vicious. As Sterling faced felony counts that could have potentially imprisoned him for more than five years, the Postal Service announced that it would pay for Skippy's funeral. Plans called for a $500 burial in a silk-lined casket at Los Angeles Pet Memorial Park with a graveside ceremony. Floral displays and a headstone were expected to add several hundred dollars more to the cost.

The Executive Branch

Instilling Security in the Troops

On October 5, 1993, nine months into his job of running the White House, Chief of Staff Thomas F. "Mack" McLarty issued a memo to "All White House Staff," asking them to inform him as to what it is that they did, what their phone numbers and titles were, and asking who it was that they reported to. Protesting to a reporter, "Of course we know what our jobs are," White House Communications Director Mark Gearan explained that it was all part of a White House management review exercise. The first revelation elicited by the memo: Staffers complained that they didn't have the time to sit down and write out responses to the eight questions.

Like Dude, Will Your Health Alliance Cover Our Short-Term Memory Loss?

When President Clinton's health care reform plan was ready to be distributed to the press, the White House decided to distribute a thousand computer disks containing the plan to the press instead of handing out a thousand copies of the 1,342-page bill. But when reporters put the disks in their computers, those with virus-alert systems were warned that the disks contained the computer virus known as Stoned III. That virus flashes the following message on a user's screen: "Your PC is stoned: LEGALIZE MARIJUANA." The White House said that the master disks were sent out of the White House for duplicating and that the virus was not on the disk when it left the White House.

- Those looking for copies of the Clinton plan had their choice of how much they wanted to spend to see it. The Government Printing Office charged $125 for a two-disk set of the Senate bill. However, the full text was available for $10 from the National Technical Information Service in Virginia. Then again, those able to log onto the Internet computer network could look at it for free. The White House put the whole plan on the network.

The White House Escort Service

In a move guaranteed to anger the press, the Clinton White House ordered that any reporters holding White House press passes who wished to go see someone in the Old Executive Office Building next to the White House must first check in at the White House press room and then be escorted to the OEOB by a White House staffer. After the reporter's business was finished, the reporter must be escorted back. According to reporting by Al Kamen in *The Washington Post*, officials at the OEOB grew so frustrated with the time-consuming procedure that they simply started telling reporters to walk into the front entrance of the OEOB, say that they were there for an appointment, not an interview, and show only their driver's licenses, not their press passes, thus circumventing the escort system.

How He Would Have Spent It If He Had Had the Chance

Among Richard Nixon's personal papers now in the National Archives is his memo to White House staff with instructions planning his state funeral, if by chance he had died while in office. Nixon would have had himself lying in state in the Capitol Rotunda for two days to allow the throngs to pass by and offer their last respects. Meanwhile, he wanted music played which ranged from patriotic songs to religious hymns. His send-off song was to be "California, Here I Come," played softly and slowly.

- On Nixon's death in 1994 President Clinton declared an official day of mourning and closed the federal government for a day, as had been done upon the deaths of former Presidents Truman, Eisenhower, and Johnson. The cost of closing the federal government for one day in 1994? More than $400 million. Of that total, $23 million was extra premium pay for "essential" workers who had to go to work anyway to keep the government functioning. They received time and a half for that day.

I'll Trade You Two Herbert Hoovers

Back in 1991 President George Bush and the (at that time) four living former Presidents (Richard Nixon, Gerald Ford, Jimmy Carter, and Ronald Reagan) all were photographed together at the dedication of the Reagan Library in Simi Valley, California. Together they signed a certain number of the photographs featuring them posed side by side and then agreed not to sign any other copies of the same photograph. That decision in effect drove up the price of the signed copies on the memorabilia market. "They're acting like baseball players," said autograph dealer Herman Darvick. He estimated that each of the fifteen hundred autographed photos is worth $5,000. According to a Bush spokesperson, there was no personal profit motive involved. "It was for them to give to whomever they wanted, to help in raising funds for each of the [presidential] libraries."

Right ... and I Want to Be the Official Food Taster

David Watkins, director of the White House Office of Administration for the Clinton administration, was forced to resign after news reports that he took the President's helicopter Marine One to travel to a private country club near Camp David, where Watkins and another aide proceeded to play golf. Amid the press reports and a widely disseminated photo of Watkins's golf foursome carrying golf bags onto the helicopter while a marine guard stood saluting, a White House spokesperson at first described the trip as a routine measure to check out the course prior to the President's playing on it himself. The official statement from the White House Military Office explained the trip as a "training mission" to familiarize the flight crew with the course and the golf game as an effort by the staff to familiarize themselves with "those aspects related to actual time of play and associated impact of security plans." Clinton later denounced the episode and said that the taxpayers would be reimbursed for the $13,000 cost of the trip.

Top Secret

Better Keep That Under Wraps! I Just Saw the Kaiser's Great-Great-Grandkids Outside . . .

It took a Freedom of Information Act request to get the National Archives in 1992 to declassify its oldest document. The subject of that document? Troop movements in Europe in 1917. It was classified "Confidential," and the official reason for its continued classification was that it was the position of the U.S. Army that its release could harm national security. It is estimated that the archives house thirty million pages of classified documents dated before 1960! As of 1993, the archives said that if they operated under normal conditions, it would take nineteen years to review and consider for declassification State Department documents stamped secret for the years 1960–63!

I Infer Something Else

The following (reprinted at the time by *The Progressive*) is part of a Pentagon report submitted to Congress in

1980 concerning the subject of arms control: "The [deleted] is a key element of the Worldwide Military Command and Control System (WWMCCS) warning network. . . . [Deleted] currently consists of [deleted] satellite; two [deleted] satellites; an [deleted] for [deleted] from the [deleted] satellite; a [deleted] for [deleted] and the [deleted] satellites; and a [deleted] which provides [deleted] for the [deleted]. . . . Using these data, [deleted] can be inferred."

Not a Moment Too Soon

Columnist Jack Anderson reported that at the close of the first year of the Clinton administration, a senior official at the Office of Management and Budget received the following letter. The envelope was stamped SPECIAL, PRIORITY, and SPECIAL HANDLING and was taped shut; inside was an envelope stamped PROPERTY OF U.S. GOVERNMENT and VIA COURIER that was taped shut; inside that was an envelope stamped SECRET three times. Inside the final envelope was a letter from a Cabinet official concerning the appointment of an aide to become a member of the President's Management Council. The council was entrusted with implementing the administration's reinventing government plans.

On Not Knowing When to Quit

When the Central Intelligence Agency's Task Force on Greater CIA Openness submitted its fifteen-page report

to CIA Director Robert Gates in 1992, it was stamped SE-
CRET. According to the classification system, that means
that the "unauthorized disclosure" of the document
could "be expected to cause serious damage to national
security." Even after Gates used the report as the basis
for a major policy speech on "a greater openness" at the
agency, requests for the report through the Freedom of
Information Act were greeted with a CIA response saying: "We determined [the report] must be withheld in its
entirety." Criticism of the classification of the report by
Congress resulted in the agency's declassifying almost
the entire document.

Lower the "Cone of Silence" Before Reading Any Further

The chairs of the Senate and House Intelligence committees, Senator Dennis DeConcini (D., Arizona) and
Representative Dan Glickman (D., Kansas), introduced
legislation in 1994 to reduce the number of documents
the government classifies and the amount of time they
must remain classified. The two lawmakers said that as
of 1994 the federal government was classifying seven
million documents each year. The classification system
in effect has four levels: confidential, secret, top secret,
and code word. At the code word level there is the potential for hundreds of more levels of classification as
documents are compartmentalized from view. That com-
partmentalization is protected by more than a hundred
"special access programs." The proposed legislation
would reduce the entire system to two levels: secret and
top secret. (As reported in *The New York Times*, a CIA-

Pentagon report on the secrecy system related the story of a Pentagon official who requested a copy of a report on "security awareness" with which he could then brief contractors. The report was an unclassified document. The request took six months to answer, and when he finally received the document, it was stamped SECRET. NOT RELEASABLE TO CONTRACTORS.)

Kafka, Call Your Office

A lawyer representing a CIA employee whom the agency was trying to fire sought to review the agency's personnel regulations. Before being allowed to read the regulations, he had to sign a secrecy agreement. He was then permitted to read the regulations and to take notes, but he was not permitted to leave with those notes. Instead he had to hand them over to agency personnel, who reviewed his notes to look for anything he had written that could jeopardize national security. The CIA then faxed the censored notes back to him. Although he was able to settle the case with what he learned, the attorney filed a Freedom of Information Act request to have the regulations released. When after two years no action was forthcoming, he filed a suit against the agency in U.S. district court. In a settlement of the suit the CIA agreed to have its personnel regulations "available for public inspection and copying." The CIA published the "notice of availability" in the *Federal Register* but didn't give a location where the documents could be reviewed. Instead it provided the name and phone number of the agency's information and privacy coordinator. This irked the lawyer since "the reason I had to file suit was that I kept calling [the CIA officer in question] and the people who

answered the phone refused to put me through to him.
I decided the only way to get their attention was to file
a lawsuit."

Fun at the FBI

A Federal Bureau of Investigations agent and his supervisor were suspended after it was learned that the agent,
while conducting a preliminary background interview of
a prominent black lawyer in Boston for a federal judge-
ship, demanded that the lawyer submit a footprint as
part of the investigation process. The agent then hung a
copy of the footprint in his office and openly joked
about his prank. The Justice Department called the behavior "entirely unacceptable and abhorrent to the
department."

- During its standoff with white separatist Randall
  Weaver in Idaho in 1992 the FBI utilized a number
  of psychological warfare techniques against the
  Weaver family. While a four-hundred-member FBI
  task force surrounded the isolated Weaver cabin,
  the agency planted microphones on the cabin over
  which it could both monitor what was going on inside and broadcast its own messages to the family.
  Early in the confrontation Weaver's thirteen-year-old
  son and forty-two-year-old wife were killed. According to court records of the case, while Mrs. Weaver's
  body lay inside with the rest of the family, the FBI
  taunted the family with messages such as "Good
  morning, Mrs. Weaver. We had pancakes for breakfast. What did you have?"

You Should See Their Decoder Rings

So secret is the National Reconnaissance Office that members of Congress are forbidden by secrecy laws to utter its name in open sessions. Although its headquarters is housed in the Pentagon, and its "black" budget is estimated at $7 billion per year, there is no official acknowledgment of the agency's existence. The NRO conducts high-tech spying, operating this country's secret spy satellites to monitor everything from troop movements to telecommunications. However, congressional criticism of the agency surfaced in 1992, after it was revealed that the Pentagon was dissatisfied with the high-tech intelligence provided during the Gulf War. The military called the satellite photographs provided by the NRO "neither timely nor adequate" and blamed them for "unnecessary" bombing of civilian targets during the fighting.

Time to Photograph the Photographers, I Say—Why? Can't Tell You Because of National Security

According to a 1992 report by John C. Layton, the inspector general for the Department of Energy, that agency regularly disseminated "intelligence information" on U.S. citizens without getting prior approval for such activity from the attorney general. Layton also revealed that the department hired a government contractor to photograph protesters at a nuclear test site in Nevada. His report said that the contractor held the negatives of the photos "for an indefinite period" in violation of department policy. In general, he found that the department never adequately informed employees about how to protect the rights of U.S. citizens while those employees were engaged in "intelligence activities."

And They Didn't See a Thing . . .

According to reporting by the *Commercial Appeal* newspaper, the U.S. Army conducted a campaign of spying against black Americans beginning during World War I and continuing at least through the Vietnam War. According to the paper's interviews of more than two hundred former Army agents, the spying, which monitored every prominent civil rights leader, involved the use of Green Berets, wiretaps, and even U-2 spy planes, used to photograph large demonstrations. The report said that the campaign started during the First World War because the Army feared that blacks would be subverted by German agents. The paper also charged that at the time of the Reverend Martin Luther King Jr.'s assassination, there were eight Green Berets in Memphis to monitor his activities.

AAACHOOO!

As part of its biological warfare program, the U.S. Army has conducted more than 170 open-air tests of bacterial agents at Dugway Proving Ground, Utah, since 1979. The base is just seventy miles away from Salt Lake City. Writing in 1988, Leonard Cole, a faculty member at Rutgers University and the author of a book on the Army's tests, charged that the Army readily admits that "from time to time" it releases *Bacillus subtillus* bacteria in Utah to simulate a germ warfare attack of a more lethal agent. During the 1950s and 1960s the Army spread some of these same bacteria in major U.S. cities to judge how well they would survive among the population.

Question Authority, Indeed

Late in 1993 the United States government admitted that it had conducted more than two hundred nuclear weapons tests in secret at a Nevada test site since the 1940s, the last in 1990. Thirty-six of those tests accidentally released radiation into the atmosphere. At the same time the Energy Department revealed that during an experiment involving plutonium in the 1940s eighteen civilians were injected with the radioactive substance to see if there was a safe dosage that workers could tolerate. None of the eighteen was aware of what they were being injected with.

- The department also revealed the existence of a program in the 1940s in which researchers at Vanderbilt University gave radioactive pills to 751 pregnant women. The women and their fetuses were exposed to radiation levels thirty times higher than natural levels. A follow-up study in the late 1960s suggested that at least three of the children born to those mothers likely died from the experiment.

- In perhaps the weirdest of the radioactivity tests, during the 1960s 102 civilians at the University of Chicago and Argonne National Laboratory actually ate fallout from the Nevada weapons test site. The saddest involved Harvard and MIT researchers who, between 1945 and 1956, gave retarded teenage boys radioactive milk for breakfast or iron tablets containing radiation levels equal to fifty chest X rays. The boys' parents were never informed of the testing.

- Among the files released on the subject was a document of a 1956 meeting of the U.S. Atomic Energy Commission at which members discussed using Pacific islanders as test subjects after nuclear test explosions in the 1950s. One scientist was quoted as saying, "While it is true that these people do not live, I would say, the way Westerners do, civilized people, it is nevertheless true that these people are more like us than the mice." The scientist in question, interviewed after the release of the document in 1994, said, "The whole thing is taken out of context. That was a two-day meeting, and as I remember, I was doing most of the talking. I may have been tired, or the stenographer may have been tired. I may just have been stupid."

- As the Energy Department was releasing those revelations, *The New York Times* reported that millions of pounds of radioactive reactor fuel is stored in twenty-nine department storage pools at three sites in the United States (Aiken, South Carolina; Richland, Washington; and Idaho Springs, Idaho). The newspaper said that the plutonium has been sitting there for so long that the containers have rusted and radioactivity is leaking.

- As part of opening up the classified files, Energy Secretary Hazel O'Leary retitled the agency's Office of Classification as the new Office of Declassification. The number of classified pages in the office totals thirty-two million, an amount that, if stacked, would measure three miles long. The office also has an eighteen-month time lag in answering requests under the Freedom of Information Act.

Now Where Did I Put That?

As part of her further declassification of Department of Energy records, Secretary Hazel O'Leary revealed late in 1993 that the Hanford Nuclear Reservation, the country's main factory for plutonium production from 1944 to 1987, produced 53 metric tons of bomb-grade plutonium and 13 metric tons of reactor-grade plutonium for a total of 66 metric tons. However, research by Dr. Thomas B. Cochran, a senior scientist at the Natural Resources Defense Council, found a discrepancy of 1.5 metric tons of plutonium according to his calculations. That's enough for three hundred nuclear weapons. Energy Department officials said that further studies have determined that the total was really 67.4 metric tons, closer to Cochran's figure. Said Cochran: "The government has never been through this accounting exercise before. That's troubling. Banks do this kind of thing once a day."

We've All Got a Secret

According to the annual report by the federal Information Security Oversight Office, in 1993 the government declassified 18,051 pages of secret information each day. However, it also classified 17,558 pages each day. For all of fiscal 1993 the government created more than 6.4 million new secrets (or 6,408,688 documents), up 1 percent from 1992. Of the 9 million pages of classified material that came up for review in 1993 the government declassified 6.6 million pages. That was 3 million fewer pages than were released in 1992.

The Greatest Deliberative Body in the World

(Oh, My God!)

Just Two Olives, Straight Up

The House Appropriations Committee instructed the Defense Department to purchase more olives during fiscal year 1994, and really big ones at that. Writing in the defense budget, the committee "directs the Defense Procurement Agency to increase its purchases of Jumbo, Colossal, and Super Colossal ripe olives in future solicitations for ripe olive purchases." Just a coincidence that Representative Vic Fazio (D., California), who represents the olive-growing region of the Sacramento Valley, sits on that committee. Just coincidence. A Fazio aide complained that in the past the Pentagon ignored the larger sizes when buying olives. Fazio also pointed out that jumbo olives cost between $300 and $400 per ton versus $685 per ton for the smaller ones.

Stop the Insanity!

During the first session of the 103d Congress 210 public laws were produced. Of that total, four dozen were commemorative resolutions passed by the Congress and signed by the President to honor certain groups or popular causes. I hope you didn't forget to celebrate "National Good Teen Day" on January 16, 1994, or "Education and Sharing Day, USA," which was observed on April 2, 1993. Besides the commemorative days, places got some honors. Fond du Lac, Wisconsin, was officially recognized as the "World Capital of Aerobatics."

- Back in 1989 one estimate said that a full third of all the legislation passed by the 100th Congress consisted of such commemorative legislation. Those resolutions have to be printed just like other laws, and staffers actually spend time to get cosignatures of as many other members as possible on each bill. If the cost in printing and time wasn't waste enough, the true absurdity is that most of these resolutions are finally signed into law days or months after the commemorative day has already passed. In the 103d Congress the bill setting aside August 1993 as "National Scleroderma Awareness Month" was signed into law in October of that year. Likewise, "Education and Sharing Day, USA," on April 2, wasn't signed until April 12.
- Early in its second session the 103d Congress voted to recognize July 28, 1994, as "National Parents Day." Sponsored by Representative Dan Burton (R., Indiana) and boasting 217 cosponsors, the resolution states: "It is in the interest of society and gov-

ernment to adopt policy that helps families stay together by strengthening and sustaining fathers and mothers in fulfilling their parental roles." And they say Congress can't make a difference in our day-to-day lives.

Oh, to Have Time on One's Hands ...

In response to the Northern Rockies Ecosystem Protection Act sponsored by Representative Carolyn Maloney from New York City, Representative Larry LaRocco (D., Idaho) introduced the Wilderness Equity Act of 1994. LaRocco was irked that Maloney's bill would designate 13 million acres in western states (4.5 million in Idaho) as wilderness areas. That designation would prevent any commercial use of the land or its resources. LaRocco's bill would so designate Central Park and the Upper East Side of Manhattan as protected wilderness areas in return. "Fair is fair," said LaRocco. "[Idahoans] feel sorry for New Yorkers. We feel that we live in heaven and people in New York might live in hell."

I Got It, We'll Give 'Em Some Money and They'll Arrange, You Know, Stuff ... Good Stuff ...

For fiscal 1994 the Senate Labor Committee added $4 million for the Dwight D. Eisenhower Leadership Development Program. Created by Senator Arlen Specter (R.)

and Representative William Goodling (R.), both of Pennsylvania, the program is designed to foster "new generations of leaders in the areas of national and international affairs." It awards grants of $175,000 to efforts to stimulate those leadership skills. Grant proposals to receive the awards have ranged from West Texas A&M University's offer to arrange for a hundred "at-risk fifth graders" to attend "Rap and Eat" encounter programs featuring the rap group Chillin' Time to Wayne State University's plan to run "leadership development seminars" that would include the "Washington International Walkabout"—students would get to walk around Washington, D.C., for a week.

No. 453 in a Continuing Series

Police records released through a lawsuit filed by a local newspaper revealed that after maintaining for months that "nothing happened" and that he was simply having a discussion about the problems of parenting the night he was found by police in a car with a convicted prostitute, Representative Ken Calvert (R., California) was involved in sexual activity when stopped by Corona, California, police officers. In the police reports Calvert was described as having his pants unzipped and trying to cover up with his shirt. Police also noted that he tried to drive away from the scene and stopped only on their third command. Calvert wasn't charged with any crime because the police witnessed none. In a statement after the embarrassing release of the police records, Calvert said, "I realize now that this, or a similar incident, was probably inevitable" because of several personal upheavals he had experienced in the fifteen months prior to the incident.

All Aboard!

The summer of 1994 witnessed the debut of the new $18 million subway line linking the Dirksen Senate Office Building and the Hart Senate Office Building with the U.S. Capitol, a building five minutes' walk from either. The cost per hundred yards of track is estimated at $1.5 million. The system consists of four trains with three cars each. They are driverless and propelled by magnets. Each train seats twenty-five passengers. To its credit, these will be the first Senate subway cars accessible by wheelchair. Senator Harry Reid (D., Nevada), no doubt referring to the use of the current Senate subway by so many tourists and others, said, "It's not the Senate's subway; it's the public's subway."

Sisyphus, Call Your Office

In November 1993 the Library of Congress held a party celebrating the three-year effort to reduce its backlog of uncataloged materials by one third. The next day the staff went back to work to catalog the remaining twenty-seven million items. With the passing of each week the library receives thirty thousand new books, magazines, videotapes, comic strips, recordings, movies, and other items to be processed.

- Well, at least they know where those items are. Early in 1994 it was revealed that the library estimates that 300,000 books are missing from its collection and it doesn't know who took them out. Library spokesperson Helen Dalrymple said that of 3,938 books out on loan to congressional staff, 2,259 are overdue. She also noted that there is "no way of collecting late fees." Of the 22,438 books out on loan at that time, 2,912 were signed out by members of Congress. Dalrymple said that none of those books was included in the missing total of 300,000. Staff members are allowed to take out a volume for sixty days before they are sent an overdue notice. Members of Congress can keep books indefinitely.

Now If They Were to Sell a Page-a-Day Version Featuring Famous Congressional Scandals, They Might Get a Handle on That Deficit Thing

For those of you who insist on getting a free wall calendar every year, each member of Congress can pass out twenty-five hundred free copies of the official U.S. Congress annual calendar. The calendar features a photo of the Capitol and lists important dates in U.S. history. The production cost of the age-old giveaway item totals $740,000. If they all are mailed out to constituents, you can add on another $2 million. The last serious attempt to discontinue this practice was led by Representative Peter Kostmayer (D., Pennsylvania) in 1977, at the time a freshman member. "There are too many calendars in

America," said Kostmayer. "This is a step towards getting rid of such clutter." Representative John McFall (D., California) then stepped forward in defense of the clutter, relating a letter he got from a schoolteacher in which she said the children in her class "learned more about the government and history of the United States from that calendar than from all other materials she had used during the year."

Free Parking for Me but Not for Thee

In April 1994 the Senate voted 53–44 to retain its free parking space privileges at Washington's National and Dulles airports. Five days after the vote the signs were changed. The originals read: "Reserved—Supreme Court Justices—Members of Congress—Diplomats." The new signs read: "Restricted Parking—Authorized Users Only." Senator John McCain (R., Arizona), sponsor of the move to do away with the reserved spaces, said, "Perhaps the new signs indicate that the defenders of this policy are uncomfortable with the public knowing for whose benefit they are excluded from these lots." An airport spokeswoman said that the sign change had been planned well before the Senate vote.

What If a Member of Congress Sent a Letter and Nobody Read It?

The congressional "franking" privilege, which allows each member of Congress use of the mail system to communicate with constituents using only his or her "signature" as a postage mark, gives each member between $140,000 and $175,000 in free mail postage annually. However, as columnist Jack Anderson pointed out, the fact that a member cannot carry over his or her unused franking amount to the next year only encourages him or her to "use it or lose it." Of thirty proposals introduced in recent years to reform the franking system, none succeeded.

Laws for Thee but Not for Me

According to a recent study by the Employment Policy Foundation, Congress is exempt from complying with the following federal employment laws it has written for the rest of us: the National Labor Relations Act, the Occupational Safety and Health Act, the Employee Retirement Income Security Act, the Federal Labor-Management Relations Act, and the Worker Adjustment and Retraining Notification Act. The Senate is exempt from the Fair Labor Standards Act and the Equal Pay Act. The House is exempt from the Age Discrimination in Employment Act and the Rehabilitation Act. Both houses are partially exempt from the Americans with

Disabilities Act, the Family and Medical Leave Act, and Title VII of the Civil Rights Act of 1964.

No Sense of Humor

When they learned of plans by the Veterans Affairs Department to pay the Capitol Steps comedy group $6,100 to entertain a breakfast meeting of senior VA medical officials, Senators John "Jay" Rockefeller (D., West Virginia) and Frank Murkowski (R., Alaska), the chairman and ranking minority member respectively of the Senate Veterans Affairs Committee, convinced the department to cancel the event. The senators called the decision to hire the entertainment, by a troupe that regularly satirizes Congress, "terribly inappropriate," saying that it should "not be done at taxpayer expense." They termed the spending of federal money for entertainment purposes "particularly galling" and suggested instead that the medical officials "travel to Georgetown and pay to be entertained by" the group.

What's Your Point?

An invitation sent out for a fund-raising reception for Representative James A. "Jimmy" Hayes (D., Louisiana) featured a family tree design on its cover. At the top of the tree was the name W. C. Fields. Two branches onto the next level listed "Laurel" and "Hardy." Three branches onto the next level connected to "Larry," "Moe," and "Curly." Four branches down to the next level featured "Groucho," "Harpo," "Chico," and "Zeppo." Multiple branches down to the next level connected to "House of Representatives." A spokesperson for the congressman said that the design was all his idea. At least one lobbyist who received the invite responded that it "makes your colleagues in the House look like buffoons."

Just Who Was in Charge of Changing the Toner?

Late in the 1980s a rat was discovered to have "eaten" the interior of a $93,000 Xerox machine in an office in the Cannon House Office Building. Weeks before the machine stopped working, office employees discovered chewed computer and telephone cables in the room and noticed that food disappeared overnight. Finally, on the day the Xerox machine broke, its door was opened to reveal a rat's nest containing shredded paper, banana peels, corncobs, and a Hostess Twinkie still sealed in a plastic bag. Even with a $10,000 trade-in the replacement machine cost the taxpayers $97,000. The rat was believed to have been poisoned days later.

Why They Call It "Politics"

As the Senate debated an "emergency supplemental appropriations" bill in early 1994, Senator John McCain (R., Arizona) stood on the Senate floor and spoke against what he termed the "pork-barrel" spending in the bill. The package contained funds for such projects as $1.4 million for research into a potato fungus and $1.3 million targeted for social aid to the Hamaku coast of Hawaii. "The American people think we're here to provide an emergency supplemental," McCain protested. Senator Robert Byrd (D., West Virginia) responded by producing two letters written to the Appropriations Committee in 1991 asking for support of Arizona highway projects. The letters were signed by McCain. "If we're going to criticize other senators because they stand up for their constituents," said Byrd, "then one should be careful not to ask for favors from the Appropriations Committee."

I Just Want the Contract to Do the Field Research

In 1991 Representative Mervyn Dymally (D., California) introduced legislation that would have established the United States Commission on Obesity. One task of the new entity would be to "study the influence of the fast-food industry on obesity and the diet habits of the United States population." The plan called for fifteen unpaid commission members, a paid director, and "additional personnel as the director considers appropriate."

Oink!

"The Pig Book" is the annual publication produced by Citizens Against Government Waste (CAGW). With its focus on "pork barrel" spending, each volume lists numerous examples of members of Congress appropriating federal money for projects of local interest to themselves. When they looked at the fiscal year 1994 appropriations bills, here's some of what they found:

- The Senate Agriculture Committee appropriated $4,443,000 for "wood utilization research." Since 1985, $27,081,000 was funneled into the research.

- The same committee spent $34,645,000 for research into screwworms, even though the worm has been eliminated from the United States. This funding is apparently directed at a program to eradicate the screwworm from southern Mexico.

- In the House the conference report on foreign operations restored "language stricken by the Senate and appropriates up to $19,600,000 for the International Fund for Ireland." As the CAGW noted, past spending on the program has used taxpayer money to pay for a golf video and pony riding centers.

- The Treasury/Postal Service bill saw the House add $2.4 million for the design and construction of a parking facility that would provide two hundred parking spaces for federal employees. However, there are only eighteen federal employees in the town where the parking facility will be built.

- An amount of $11.5 million was set aside to modernize a power plant at the Philadelphia naval yard, a facility scheduled to be closed.

- Money was added to help fund a five-car, two-mile transit system in Orlando, a project that may total $42 million and won't be complete until at least 2010. The CAGW noted that a free bus shuttle currently covers the same area.

Reality Bites

During a 1993 debate on the Family Planning Amendments Act, Representative Gerald Solomon (R., New York) became angry when Representative Louise Slaughter (D., New York) tried to cut him off on the House floor. "You had better not do that," said Solomon. "You will regret that as long as you live. Who do you think you are?" If you were lucky enough to be watching C-SPAN again, that's what you saw and heard. In the *Congressional Record*, where lawmakers can change the reality of what they actually said, Solomon was quoted as expressing "the greatest respect" for Slaughter, whom he referred to as "the gentlelady." He also expressed "hope that she or any other Member not try to cut off another Member."

I Give Up—It's Either the Penguin in *Batman 2* or the Witch in *The Wizard of Oz*

In another slip of the supposed decorum that governs Capitol Hill, Senator Alan Simpson (R., Wyoming) spoke on the Senate floor about three House supporters of legislation to raise fees on ranchers whose cattle graze on federal land. Simpson called Representative Ralph Regula (R., Ohio) a "shabby rascal" and referred to him and Representatives Mike Synar (D., Oklahoma) and George Miller (D., California) as "absolutely obsessed. They go to bed at night and they think about grazing fees. It is on their brain, seared through there. . . . When you have the hook and the hammer in your hand and use it, remember, it will come to pass that you will be the one pleading one day. This is a jackboot on the neck, and they are having a lot of fun with it. And I am going to have a lot of fun with them."

- The rules of Senate decorum and other procedures are contained in the sixteen-hundred-page *Riddick's*

Senate Procedure, a one-volume guide to Senate practices and precedents. While it does tell a senator how to cut off a debate, it also lists traditional regulations that must be observed, such as the one that says a senator cannot lean on a podium during a debate. Said author Floyd Riddick, the Senate parliamentarian emeritus: "If you don't have a framework setting up a way of doing business, you can get lost in the barnyard." Okay. The House version of its procedure is ten volumes long.

- Speaking of decorum, the sometimes antiquated parliamentary rules in effect in Congress often get in the way of the nation's business. When Representative Kweisi Mfume (D., Maryland) tried to condemn remarks made by Senator Ernest "Fritz" Hollings (D., South Carolina) that he deemed to be racially insensitive, Mfume was forbidden by the rules even to mention Hollings by name. Mfume was reduced to referring to Hollings as "a gentleman of the other body" and "a person who resides in the state of South Carolina." Representative G. V. "Sonny" Montgomery (D., Mississippi) interrupted Mfume at that point to remind him that "he cannot refer to members of the other body and statements made by that member." Mfume said that he was "not necessarily mentioning a member of the other body, but a resident of the state of South Carolina."

How to Make Every Kid Want to Read the *Congressional Record*

In perhaps the most blunt comment on the words offered in the *Congressional Record*, Arkansas Governor Jim Guy Tucker vetoed a bill calling on state educators to post the *Record* in public schools. Tucker commented that the *Record* contained "bizarre polemics on religious and political positions, as well as excerpts from other documents, that Arkansas parents would be startled and appalled to have foisted upon their children—particularly in the lower grades."

My God, Holmes! You Mean, They're Only Interested in Playing Politics?

The newsletter *CongressDaily* reprinted the following remarks of retiring Senator George Mitchell (D., Maine) reflecting on what's wrong with the greatest deliberative body in the world (while he was making a speech to an industry trade group): "I remember [former Senator John Stennis, D., Mississippi] telling me that, when he first came to the Senate, there were about 70 roll call votes a year. Now, of course, we have several hundred a year, large numbers of them having no legislative purpose. They are intended to get the other side on record on an issue that's controversial and can be used in a campaign. They are intended for use in fund-raising appeals with direct mass mailings. . . . They're intended to express views on a wide range of issues that are topical, and therefore enable one to get television attention."

A Short Trip Around Just a Few of the Agencies

Aww! Do We Have To?

Weeks after coming on board as the new head of the Forest Service, Jack Ward Thomas issued a memo to agency personnel concerning the six messages that he intended to stress to "help communicate the direction" of the agency. Included were: "Obey the law," "Tell the truth," and "Trust and make use of our hard-working expert work force." Duh.

- In the late 1980s the Forest Service sought to consolidate its staff by moving employees to a central downtown office. After the plan was approved and the $14 million renovation of the building was begun, however, someone noticed that the eight hundred employees who would be moved would have to share ten parking spaces. Apparently when the plan was first conceived, there was plenty of parking near the new site. During the intervening years

the existing parking lots were taken over by somebody else. The renovation continued, as did the service's plan to move, but some workers originally
scheduled for relocation were forced to stay at their
existing locations.

- While we're speaking of the Forest Service: Back in
  1987 a series of rock carvings were discovered in
  the Siskiyou National Forest in Oregon. The carvings, on three boulders, appeared to be primitive
  petroglyphs and were immediately preserved and
  examined by several archaeologists both in and out
  of the Forest Service. In the next few years the
  government began construction of an interpretive
  center in the forest to explain to tourists the significance of the ancient artwork. Work on the center
  had to be stopped however when artist Jeff Kerker
  stepped forward and explained how he had drawn
  the petroglyphs fifteen years earlier. "I wasn't trying
  to fool anyone. I was interested in how long it might
  take to make them. All it took was one afternoon,"
  said Kerker.

And Just What Customs Are Those?

A House Ways and Means Committee oversight investigation into U.S. Customs Service practices in 1990 reported that in several instances Customs personnel
inspected cargo by cutting it open with chain saws. In
the two cases cited, a teakwood elephant and a container of paper products were totally destroyed. While
the service denied the use of chain saws, inspectors
from the committee found one at an agency facility in
Seattle. Agency officials then admitted to other locations

where chain saws were also used. The report, listing sixteen critical findings on how the service conducts business, also determined that the agency had "little or no
incentive to avoid damaging cargo during examinations."

Social Security! Please Hold for the Next Few Days ... An Automated Voice Will Be with You Shortly ...

Late in 1993 the Social Security Administration revealed
that it was considering improving its response time on
its toll-free telephone lines by employing federal prisoners to answer the phones. The agency receives eighty
million calls per year. SSA spokesperson Phil Gambino
said, "[The agency] is committed to providing world-
class telephone service to the American public, answering every call on the first attempt. To accomplish this
self-imposed goal within the current fiscal environment,
we must think creatively." The prisoners would be paid
between 42 cents and $1.05 per hour.

Forget Operators; Hire Some Accountants

According to a report by the General Accounting Office, between 1981 and 1986 more than four million recipients of Social Security checks were paid the wrong amounts. Overpayments averaged $1,069 while underpayments averaged $591.

That's "Internal," Not "Infernal" (So, Like, Can We Be Just 89 Percent Accurate on Our Returns?)

According to a congressional report, only one out of every four callers actually got through to an Internal Revenue Service office during the period of January 2 to April 24. It was also revealed that during 1993 the IRS answered 89 percent of taxpayers' questions accurately, up from only 63 percent right in 1989.

The Only Sure Things in Life Are ... Uh, Well, Okay ... the Only Sure Thing in Life Is Taxes

Iranian immigrant Ehsanolla Motaghed, sixty-six, was indicted in April 1990 for allegedly offering an IRS agent a $4,000 cash bribe during a tax investigation. At his arraignment it was charged that Motaghed had assets of nearly $1 million and had invested heavily in Treasury bills. He in fact posted $110,000 bail in Treasury bills. The review of his 1985, 1986, and 1987 tax returns led the IRS to claim that he owed $156,000 in back taxes. Less than two months later Motaghed died of sclerosis. Two months after that the IRS filed liens against his estate for the tax bill, and federal prosecutors were considering the exhumation of his body to prove that it was Motaghed in the grave. Within weeks IRS agents grilled Motaghed's daughter about the death. Although she had no doubt that her father was dead and the death certificate identified him and the medical cause of his death, the prosecutors were still heading toward the exhumation. The attorney for the estate noted that under Nebraska law the only legal basis to allow an exhumation is to dissect a body to determine cause of death. "They would have to dig him up for the purpose of dissection," he said. "I've heard the IRS does that to people while they're still alive, but not when they're dead."

Look, I'm Not Inferring Anything—Really!

In 1991 managers of the cafeteria in the Treasury Department building issued a memo on the condition of the cafeteria's silverware. Of the 2,040 individual pieces it owned, a full 70 percent (1,430 pieces) was missing and presumed stolen. That building is, of course, where the IRS is located. But I don't mean to infer anything.

Computer Errors You'd Never Get Away With

In the midst of trying to collect $2 million in back taxes from federal prison inmate Joseph H. Hale, the IRS made a "computer error" and instead sent Hale a check for $359,380.25. Then, after Hale didn't return the money, a federal grand jury charged that a friend of Hale's helped him dispose of the cash and indicted them both. After two years the IRS found only $55,558.34. "It was a mistake," said an IRS spokesperson. "It was a computer mistake. Apparently a claim for refund was filed, and apparently it was honored. A refund somehow went out." At the time Hale was imprisoned for fraud in an unrelated matter.

- Early in 1994 the IRS admitted that a computer program it was using to review tax returns in search of cheaters was in fact rejecting numerous returns from honest taxpayers who had filed electronically. The problem arose when the IRS decided to check on taxpayers claiming earned income credit to find if the dependents they listed actually existed. The agency got a magnetic tape from the Social Security Administration listing the names and birth dates of millions of people. The SSA claims that when the IRS programmed its computers to cross-reference returns to the SSA tape, the computer was unable to read zeros in the dates of birth of the dependents and automatically rejected each return where that problem came up. "All the [dependents] rejected are people who have a zero in the date of birth," said an SSA spokesperson. According to one tax service that files electronic returns for clients, on the basis of its experience, the number of incorrectly rejected returns nationwide was probably more than a hundred thousand. The IRS said it had no way to know how many were involved.

- The IRS said that electronic tax return filing has grown to account for 40 percent of all its detected fraudulent returns in 1993. However, the gap between what is owed by taxpayers and what's actually paid has grown to $150 billion annually. The agency believes that this situation is directly related to the fact that the rate of audited returns is at less than 1 percent. "That's the dilemma," said an agency spokesperson. "The detection is going up, but we're not sure what that's indicative of." The IRS is now using supercomputers at Los Alamos National Laboratory that had formerly been involved in nuclear weapons research to review returns for patterns of fraud.

Accounting as Performance Art

According to a report in *The New York Times*, the IRS "wrote a one-year grace period" into the enforcement of new regulations governing how workers receiving free parking from their employers have to pay income taxes on the value above $155 per month. The law, which was supposed to go into effect with 1993 taxes, was designed to conserve energy by discouraging workers from driving themselves to work. Taxpayers were supposed to follow rules on how to calculate taxable fringe benefits when dealing with the parking space matter. However, the regulation contained a transition rule that for 1993 taxes only allowed taxpayers to ignore the fringe benefit calculations and just use "reasonable good faith" methods to determine taxes owed. The agency utilized its own "good faith" in calculating just how much money the seventy highest-ranking IRS officials owed for their indoor, reserved, free parking spaces at the headquarters building. In a city where most similar spaces would cost $300 per month, it used a method of calculation based on the fee of $6.93 per square foot of parking garage that it is charged by the General Services Administration. The calculation came to an amount less than $155 per month, thus allowing its executives not to owe any such tax. Said a spokesperson: "This particular method we used for evaluation, a good faith method, is a method any taxpayer could have used."

I Guess They'll Find Out

A wildfire study by the Bureau of Land Management that involved starting a five-acre fire at the Malheur National Wildlife Refuge near Frenchglen, Oregon, went awry as the fire jumped a fire line and burned nine hundred acres, including a bird habitat. The theory being tested was whether worms and other invertebrates emerge earlier in the year from burned land.

The Dance of Bureaucracy

Complaining that a top-heavy management system was putting his agency in "paralysis," Bureau of Reclamation Commissioner Dan Beard announced plans to streamline what was once the world's largest builder of giant dams. He said that the agency's huge staff levels and antiquated organizational structure would be changed. Among the targets in the reduction in personnel was the agency's Denver office, which Beard fingered as indicative of a top-heavy bureaucracy. As evidence of the problems, bureau officials recounted the story of the attempt to gain approval for a temperature control system for Shasta Dam in northern California. The system was designed to alleviate the effects of the dam on salmon in the region. The approval process began during the Carter administration in 1977. Along the way that one system gained more than four hundred approvals. As of late 1993 construction of the system had still not begun.

The "Interim" Always Gets You

Two thousand acres of oceanfront property on Coos Bay, Oregon, were three days away from being put off-limits to mineral claims for five years when a convicted felon laid claim to the land. The land had been under a two-year order from the Interior Department banning mineral claims, but it expired on March 8, 1993. The ban was set to be renewed by a five-year ban, but that didn't take effect until April 29, 1993. In the interim the applicant acted and got the land. As Jack Anderson reported, the applicant later sold the mineral rights for 790 acres, part of the Oregon Dunes National Seashore, to a friend he had met while they were both in prison. The land reportedly contains pure silica, a component of glass manufacturing. "We've been apologizing quite profusely for this one," said a Bureau of Land Management spokesperson.

What? Was Spielberg Doing It?

The construction and interest costs of building the visitors' center at Hoover Dam are expected to reach $119 million before it opens. Congress originally appropriated $32 million for the building in 1984, but costs rose with no apparent oversight. Dan Beard, who took office in 1994 as the commissioner for the Bureau of Reclamation, called the project "a tragedy." "It destroys the credibility of federal agencies," he said. Beard did do his part to halt any further extravagance. He refused to authorize production of a twelve-minute film that would have been shown at the visitors' center. The film's projected cost: $1.7 million.

The Census: Don't Let This Happen to Your Town

The town of Secretary, Maryland, was ignored by the 1980 census, receiving none of the federal questionnaires. So a Census Bureau spokesperson called it a "very unfortunate coincidence" when in 1990 the town was again ignored. The spokesperson assured the town that it would be counted, laying the blame on the post office. The post office in turn laid blame right back at the Census Bureau. "If they don't provide us the forms, we can't deliver them," said a postal spokesperson.

Rules for Thee but Not for Me

When Rodney Smith, deputy executive director of the President's Commission on Organized Crime, sat down at the witness table to testify at a hearing of the House Post Office and Civil Service Committee in 1986, he was asked by the committee chairman, Representative Gary Ackerman (D., New York), to give a urine specimen. Smith had come to testify about the commission's plan to institute mandatory drug testing for all federal workers. As an aide put a plastic bottle on the table, Ackerman said, "The chair will require you to go to the men's room under the direct observation of a male member of the subcommittee staff to urinate in this specimen bottle." Smith refused, calling it "a cheap stunt." Ackerman pointed out that under the commission's proposal, federal workers wouldn't be warned either of a surprise drug test.

I Just Had No Idea Things Were So Bad

By June 1994 the Federal Communications Commission planned to have ten cars cruising the streets of America, each loaded with $75,000 worth of equipment to detect unlicensed radio signals and signals causing interference. Each car contains two computers, a mobile phone, a color printer, and a satellite receiver in the trunk. The FCC plans one day to have a total of seventy such cars, two for each of its thirty-five field offices. The agency said that it usually detects two or three pirate radio signals each month.

Fun in Our National Parks: TweedleDee

In 1986 the National Park Service paid $230,000 for a half acre of land in Southwest Washington, D.C. The service bought the land at a General Services Administration surplus property auction. Two years later a private real estate title search revealed that the Park Service had already owned some of the land it bought. It had originally been purchased back in 1914.

Hey, Beavis, Isn't That "Civil War" Thing Over Yet?

In 1989 National Park Service rangers caught a person dressed as a Confederate fifer in an officially sanctioned Civil War reenactment event at the Antietam National Battlefield in Sharpsburg, Maryland, exiting a bathroom marked "Ladies." Unmasking the soldier, they discovered that it was a woman dressed as a male. The rangers ruled her behavior inappropriate and said that she could not participate in the exercise dressed as a soldier. The woman, who has studied the Civil War extensively, claims that she has identified sixty-six women who fought as men during the conflict. A park historian went so far as to note that "perhaps two or three" women were among 126,000 combatants in the fighting in question on September 17, 1862, making the female presence only 3/126,000 or 0.00238 percent. The rangers said that she could participate only if she dressed as a woman. She complied but later filed legal briefs against the Park Service and a federal lawsuit asking for a change in policy. The woman, who binds her breasts and wears her hair short when in costume, said in a deposition, "In normal civilian life I have been mistaken for a man because I'm a fairly authoritative person. I have been called 'Mister' very often." In his deposition, Park Service ranger Ted Alexander said, "She appeared to be a female, with larger hips and also breasts." He called her uniform "below our standards. It was obviously not the proper cut.

The weave was debatable." The woman's attorney estimated that with the case pending in a U.S. district court, the federal government had at that point spent tens of thousands of dollars defending its action in the case. Said the woman's husband: "If my wife portrayed a Civil War soldier, it's not going to cause the downfall of American civilization." Our Park Service apparently disagrees.

Too Much Time on His Hands

In 1994, two weeks before announcing a 25 percent personnel cut in the agency's central and regional offices and an employment freeze, National Park Service Director Roger Kennedy tried to get his top assistants to create a job for a young man he was recommending. In his memo, reprinted in part by *Washington Post* reporter Al Kamen, Kennedy wrote: "Surely we must be able to find a use for a Swahili-speaking person who has Peace Corp[s] experience, is a cum laude in English from Harvard and has a biological background in data manipulation. . . . Unfortunately, [the person] is white, which is too bad. Would you let me know if you see any prospects?"

- Earlier Kennedy had issued a memo to seventy-nine senior officials concerning the drafting of letters for his signatures. His instructions included: "1. Please do not split infinitives. Adverbs should go before the infinitive or after the infinitive but not in the midst thereof" and "2. Please eschew the word 'issue' except when it is used to mean a matter about which there is a sharp division of views. Otherwise, the word 'subject' or the word 'matter' are [*sic*] more conveniently deployed."

Sounds Pretty Stoned to Me

According to a review of profiles used to target drug couriers at airports, a defense attorney discovered that Drug Enforcement Agency procedures differ from state to state. DEA agents in Illinois operate under the assumption that the first people off the plane are in a hurry and thus should be watched as suspicious people. DEA agents in Michigan are told to watch the last people getting off a plane because they are obviously trying to appear nonchalant. DEA agents in Ohio have been told that suspects getting off a plane in the middle of a crowd may be trying to lose themselves in that crowd. Another guideline for DEA agents on weighing suspicious characters is the city of origin or destination favored by drug couriers. Unfortunately just about every major American city was eventually added to the list. The same agent, in different court testimony, said that he stopped one suspect because he "walked quickly" through an airport and in the other case stopped a man who "walked with intentional slowness."

Money for Nothin'

Despite the presence of a standing army and the fact that millions of reservists stand ready to fight and can easily be called to duty, the Selective Service System still exists. In 1994 the Department of Defense concluded that the registration system could be suspended "without irreparable damage to national security." Each year the system registers between 1.5 million and 1.75 million eighteen-year-olds for the nonexistent draft. The service's annual budget totals $24 million. Nationwide its full-time work force is only 230 people. President Clinton rejected the Pentagon proposal, instead following the recommendation of the National Security Council that registration continue. He asked Congress for $23 million for the Selective Service for 1995.

Speaking of Turkeys

A congressional panel criticized the Agriculture Department after it was revealed that federal meat inspectors launched surprise inspections of turkey processing plants a month before Thanksgiving 1993 but that the department didn't plan to issue a report on its findings until after the holiday. "If you're going to put out warnings or tell the results of the inspections, wouldn't it be wise to do it prior to the season when you have the highest consumption?" asked Representative John Mica (R., Florida). An assistant secretary of the department said that the inspection tour had "nothing to do with the season of the year," despite the fact that the agency issued a press release touting the inspections about two weeks before the holiday.

Our Nation's Change Bank

The New York Times reported on the difficulty anyone would have in trading in pennies for paper currency at the Federal Reserve Bank's Manhattan office. The exchange window is open only from 9:00 A.M. to 3:00 P.M. weekdays; one must produce two pieces of identification, one with a photo; and the redemption limit for coins to bills is limited to only $25 per person.

But They Needed to Prove to the Savings and Loans That They Knew All About Wasting Other People's Money

Back in 1992, at a time when the Federal Deposit Insurance Corporation and the Resolution Trust Corporation were asking Congress for more tax dollars to deal with the savings and loan problem, Representative Frank Annunzio (D., Illinois), a House Banking subcommittee chairman, examined the spending records of both agencies. Among other troubling findings, he noted expense records such as $3,098 for thirty-six coffee mugs and twelve T-shirts ($64.50 per item) and $1,800 for two breast pumps.

And Just Where Do They Get That?

The National Institute of Standards and Technology sells freeze-dried urine containing marijuana samples so that laboratories can calculate the accuracy of their urine-testing equipment. Three jars sell for $159.

A Gun Is a Terrible Thing to Waste

Established soon after the Spanish-American War, the government's National Board for the Promotion of Rifle Practice was intended to improve the shooting skills of potential draftees. Still funded at an annual budget of $3 million, the board lends weapons and provides free ammo to gun clubs and the Boy Scouts.

Take One Home as a Souvenir

Next time you're at the Grand Canyon, try to determine which of the boulders at its bottom are government-bought fakes. The U.S. Geological Survey wanted to disguise a water-sampling station at the base of the canyon, so it paid Cemrock Landscapes Inc. $6,000 to install two fake boulders down there. The fake rocks are made from polyester and fiberglass. They are hollow and stand four and five feet high.

Good Ideas Gone Bad

In 1988 the Tennessee Valley Authority decided to drop its employee suggestion program because the operating costs of the program amounted to more than was saved by implementing the suggestions. Of about a thousand suggestions received by the TVA, forty-six led to savings of about $580,000. Ten percent of those savings went for bonuses paid to the originators of the ideas. The agency spent about $700,000 administering the program, including $514,000 in staff expense. "The idea of the program was good, but what we ended up with was a bureaucratic, convoluted system that took so long to review the suggestions that it proved to be ineffective," said Sue Wallace, then acting director of the TVA's human resources department. One part of the bureaucratic system was a two-inch-thick handbook of rules specifying who and what would be included in the program to qualify for the bonuses.

- The following year the TVA laid off fifty-five hundred workers and cut $300,000 from its own budget in order to avoid a rate increase. Soon after that the agency spent $28,000 for a new logo designed to bolster employee morale and help it stay competitive with other utilities. "Obviously, a consistent and single identity is important to our competitiveness because people will identify better with the company, and the employees will identify better with us," said a TVA spokesperson.

No Doubt Just What Every Agency Strives For

In testimony before a Senate committee in early 1994 Charles Bowsher, head of the General Accounting Office, announced that the entire Department of Housing and Urban Development was added to the GAO's list of seventeen "high risk" agencies or programs that will draw special attention from the GAO because they are losing so much money. It was the first time an entire Cabinet-level agency attained the distinction. According to the GAO, its definition of "high risk" means that there is the possibility that tax dollars will be lost to waste, fraud, abuse, or mismanagement. Bowsher described HUD as "an organizational structure that blurs accountability; inadequate information and financial management systems ... [whose] staff [is] without the skills needed to effectively manage programs." (What else is on the GAO list? you ask. It includes the Resolution Trust Corporation, the EPA's Superfund program, the U.S. Customs Service, Internal Revenue Service receivables, and NASA contract management, among others.)

Why Not Just Combine the Smoking Lounges and the Fitness Center?

In 1993, on the heels of Vice President Al Gore's efforts to downsize government, the Federal Energy Regulatory Commission requested $80 million to build a new office complex. The total annual FERC budget is only $146.5 million, and it consists of only twelve hundred employees. According to reporting by Jack Anderson, the proposed building plan included several luxuries such as a $91,000 fitness center, $64,000 for two locker rooms, $31,000 for nine smoking lounges (at a time when the federal government is considering banning smoking in all federal buildings), five private kitchens and baths for $83,000, and two escalators for $90,000. As Anderson noted, the FERC spent $1 million to build a day-care center in its current building but initially enrolled only six children.

Jerry Lewis in *The Absent-Minded Glowing Professor*

In 1988 the Department of Energy instructed all of its contractors to inventory all classified documents in their possession. As of 1993, the Lawrence Livermore nuclear research laboratory was still searching for ten thousand classified papers concerning nuclear weapons research. Livermore told congressional investigators in 1990 that the papers were not missing but had just been "misfiled." It has at least five hundred thousand classified documents in its possession.

- When it began searching through its own files on secret radiation tests that were conducted on unwitting Americans, the Department of Energy discovered that hundreds of its files and artifacts from those experiments are themselves contaminated with radioactive dust. It is believed that scientists working on the projects contaminated their papers simply by handling them.

911 Is a Joke!

The grand opening of the federal government's new $20 million Indian Health Service hospital in Pine Ridge, South Dakota, had to be delayed for three months when officials realized that they had forgotten to plan for and install a telephone system in the building. The hospital director said that those overseeing construction had been "distracted."

Hey! Who Keeps Putting All That Work Stuff on the Computer System?

Investigators for the Department of Veterans Affairs found of the 1,449 files on the department's computer bulletin board, 500 were nongovernmental and "obviously not for official use." Included in the mix were 179 computer games, personal finance programs, genealogy lessons, info on movies and celebrities, and 19 photos of "models in swimwear." Said a VA spokesperson: "There were just women in bathing suits. Nothing nude or in compromising positions.

Intergovernmental Relations 101

In 1990 the Colorado Department of Health charged the U.S. Drug Enforcement Agency with violating state air pollution standards when it burned a half ton of seized cocaine. The DEA was formally issued a "notice of violation" for burning the drug in the Lakewood suburb of Denver. Said a DEA spokesperson: "What do they think we're going to do with it—ship it back to Colombia?"

Facts Behind the Stereotypes

When Vice President Al Gore's reinventing government project quizzed federal bureaucrats about what part of the system was most in need of reform, the overwhelming response was the rules by which government employees can be fired. Under the current regulations supervisors cannot easily dismiss workers for nonperformance. Besides civil service regulations that protect them, government employees can file discrimination claims with the Equal Employment Opportunity Commission. As of 1993 the EEOC had a backlog of seventeen thousand federal complaints, with an average age of 379 days each. Among the dozens of stranger anecdotes concerning EEOC complaints filed by government workers is the one about the biologist who, though eligible for retirement, won reinstatement to his position despite the fact that he was taking four months to complete tasks performed in two days by his colleagues. It was determined that his supervisors had failed to define the term "too slow" for him. The fact that so many such complainants are reinstated or at least win negotiated settlements has led some supervisors to transfer workers before firing them. When a Labor Department legal secretary reprimanded a part-time worker for falling behind in her filing job, the part-time worker hit the secretary, breaking her jaw. Instead of being fired, the part-time worker was transferred into a permanent position which came with a raise of $3,890. Commenting on the current state of federal employment, James B. King, director of the Office of Personnel Management, said, "If you pass your probationary period, you have a job, as a matter of law, for as long as you want it."

Son of Swine Flu Shots

The federal government's efforts to convert to the metric system of measurement, initiated in 1977, is still alive. Beginning January 1, 1994, all federal construction projects must be designed using the metric system. The National Institute of Standards and Technology, the agency in charge of the conversion, hired a construction firm to build its new buildings according to metric measure. A NIST official noted that "obviously, a lot of products used in the construction industry in this country are not in metric yet."

- NIST is also behind a move to promote a new standard size for a sheet of paper according to metric measurement. Instead of 8½ by 11 inches, NIST has endorsed a size called "A4." The new size is equivalent to 8.3 by 11.7 inches.
- Early in 1994 the Federal Highway Administration

began seeking comments on a plan to change road signs to the metric system. The choices being considered were replacing miles with kilometers over seven years; making the change in one year along with an education program; giving the states two years to change all signs to display both miles and kilometers; or just leaving the whole thing alone. (1 mile = 1.609 kilometers.)

- President Gerald Ford signed the Metric Conversion Act in 1975. In 1977 several states began changing mileage signs to kilometers along highways, but loud public opposition forced them to back down and abandon the project. In 1982 the U.S. Metric Board, established in 1977 to promote the concept, was disbanded as a money-saving move. As of the late 1980s the United States, Liberia, and Burma were the only countries in the world that had still not gone metric. The first step toward putting us back on course came with passage of the Omnibus Trade and Competitiveness Act of 1988. The trade act designated the metric system as the preferred measure for trade and commerce and required agencies of the federal government to begin adopting the system as of 1992 whenever they found it practical to do so. Representative George E. Brown, Jr., (D., California) called the bill the "strongest pro-metric legislation ever enacted in U.S. history." According to Brown, "Our strategy was to downplay the metric language in order to avoid confrontation with those who might oppose the measure without fully understanding its provisions."

Warehouse Roulette

In 1994 investigators for the U.S. Agency for International Development discovered that despite efforts at reform, agency money was still being wasted in several foreign countries. In Egypt the investigators found two warehouses containing 246 motorcycles and high-tech irrigation equipment. According to reporting by Jack Anderson, the motorcycles, $537,000 worth, were unusable in that country because licensing procedures for their operation had never been completed. The irrigation equipment wasn't being used because no one working on the irrigation project had been instructed on how to use it. The investigators reported that AID personnel explained that they were "afraid" to try to use it for fear of damaging the $138,000 equipment. Other wasteful situations were found to partly be the work of foreign governments. In Cameroon, AID spent $24 million to build university buildings, but the government refused to spend $2 million to install water systems in the structures. AID spent $12 million educating Tunisian students in the United States. More than seventy earned doctorate degrees at the expense of United States tax dollars. The program was designed to educate the students and then have them return to their homeland to put their newfound knowledge to work. Unfortunately the students never went back, and the Tunisian government made no effort to remedy the situation.

- When the Federal Deposit Insurance Corporation acquires collateral from failed banks, it goes into storage at its warehouses. Among the possessions of the agency are: forty thousand dog costumes (for humans to wear), nine thousand "Calypso Cup Holders"; a ten-foot wooden giraffe; a nude dance bar; a patent on a process for turning manure into cattle feed; and Bear Island, Minnesota (the last not stored in a warehouse).

When the Government Says You're Dead, Part II: Our Lives Are All Hanging by a Missed Keystroke at OPM

Seventy-nine-year-old Edna May Rissmiller of Laureldale, Pennsylvania, couldn't get her monthly pension check because the government declared her dead. The action also terminated her insurance coverage. With the help of her son, Mrs. Rissmiller found out that the Office of Personnel Management, which provides the Treasury Department with a list of living Americans each month, had accidentally deleted her from the list. That set in motion the chain of events declaring her dead. When the bank wouldn't take Mrs. Rissmiller's word for it over the phone, her son had to get a signed affidavit to prove that she was still very much alive. As for her insurance company, Mr. Rissmiller said, "I called them this morning, and they still say she's dead."

Jobs We Should All Have

- The United States Battle Monuments Commission has 11 members, a staff of 380, and an annual budget of $20 million. The 11 don't get a salary, but they do get several all-expenses-paid trips to Washington each year and usually an annual trip to examine monument sites in Europe or the Pacific.
- An employee at the U.S. Forest Service oversees the trademark the government holds on Smokey Bear, acting, in effect, as the character's manager. As of 1989, the position paid $42,000 per year.
- At the Pentagon there is a person directing the U.S. Army's Civilian Marksmanship Program. According to the military, this program is budgeted millions of dollars every year to train the populace "so they can function in the national interest in case of war"— i.e., teach them to shoot straight. The program, in place since 1903, dispenses about 40 million rounds of ammunition annually, free of charge. During congressional debate about finally killing this program in 1993, Representative Randy Cunningham (R., California) defended it as an anticrime program that would get "kids off the streets" (and I guess inside, training with guns, where they're supposed to be). Representative Gerald Solomon (R., New York) called it a "vital, vital program." The House voted 242–190 to preserve it. Then it garnered 67 votes in the Senate to live on till another day. Funding for 1995 was set at $2.5 million.
- Since 1976 Douglas Patton has held a nonvoting seat on the Federal Election Commission. He is one

of two special deputies (one from the House, one from the Senate) who represents the interests of the U.S. Congress on the panel. As of 1993 his salary was at least $108,234 each year, and it came with a nice office, a secretary, and an assistant. However, in 1993 a U.S. court of appeals ruled that the inclusion of an employee of Congress on the FEC, which, of course, is entrusted with regulating campaign finance laws, is a violation of the separation of powers. Thus for months (at this writing), while Patton waits for the Supreme Court to decide his fate, he has been unable to participate in commission hearings and other confidential FEC matters. Amid partisan congressional wrangling over just how Patton was filling his workdays in the interim, the FEC staff director told a reporter, "He seems very busy. But the assurance I can give you is that he's not busy on matters he ought not be busy on."

- Under terms of a U.S.-Russian arms control treaty in effect until 2001, teams from both countries live near nuclear missile plants in their counterpart's country. Thus thirty U.S. observers live immediately outside the Votkinsk Machine Building Factory in a remote part of Russia. They must enforce treaty conditions that no SS-20s or other medium-range missiles roll out of that plant. The observers live in four two-story cinder-block buildings. They are constantly shadowed by Russian security personnel and can't leave the area without asking permission. Even then they can't go farther than thirty miles. It is winter nine months out of the year there. However, the Pentagon pays for their living expenses, and their salaries (ranging from $38,000 to $75,000) are tax-exempt. Work schedules are six to nine weeks on and then six to nine weeks off. They are provided with recreational activities, television lounges, and a thirteen-hundred-film videocassette library. And they usually only have to inspect one or two missiles each month.

- The United States Board of Geographic Names is headquartered in the office of the U.S. Geological Survey in Reston, Virginia. As the overseer of the National Geographic Names Data Base, the board tracks all place-names in this country and has the final say in disputes over such names or the designation of new names. Representatives from the Postal Service, the Library of Congress, the Government Printing Office, and the departments of Commerce, Interior, and Agriculture meet monthly to hold hearings and rule on new names.

- As part of its efforts to cut costs, the Clinton administration eliminated 284 federal advisory committees early in 1994. Then Office of Management and Budget Director Leon E. Panetta (now White House chief of staff) said that the cuts would save about $17 million. In most cases the panels' members are paid on a per diem rate or by an annual allowance. Gone are such choice job opportunities as: the Board of Tea Experts (in business since 1897 to smell and taste imported teas), the United States Commission on Improving the Effectiveness of the United Nations, the Technical Advisory Group for Cigarette Fire Safety, the Scientific Advisory Group on Effects, the Civil War Sites Advisory Commission, the Advisory Panel for Political Science, and the Drinking Water Disinfection By-Products Rule Negotiated Rulemaking Advisory Committee.

Classics

In an attempt to put the rest of this book in perspective, consider the following: Back in the 1880s one of the big problems facing Congress was not the deficit but the surplus. The federal treasury had an enormous surplus, so Congress debated endlessly about what that meant about their method of governing and what should be done with it or about it. The surplus was growing at the rate of $100 million or more each year through the decade. In fact, each year during the period 1866 to 1893 there was a federal revenue surplus. House historians in the late 1980s, preparing for the upcoming bicentennial of the House, looked back at this curious time and found that the Forty-ninth Congress concluded that the surplus was "largely a product of the high tariffs that allegedly protected growing industries and maintained the relatively high wages of American workers." The House historians concluded that the whole problem of what to do evaporated along with the surplus during the depression of the 1890s. However, in the interim, they noted that the supporters of the tariffs in Congress "absorbed the surplus with pork-barrel projects for their home districts." Uh-oh.

Schemes to spend tax dollars by the 1960s are eerily familiar to anyone who's read a newspaper in the past fifteen years. Consider the following, originally reported in *Saga* magazine:

- In the mid 1960s the federal government purchased a million acres of dry land that ran through Minnesota and North and South Dakota. The Interior Department's Sport, Fisheries, and Wildlife Bureau (now Fish, Wildlife, and Parks) spent $105 million to transform the land with water projects like dams and ponds in order to create a marshland home for migratory ducks, which prior to that I guess slept in motels.
- The National Science Foundation gave a zoology professor $28,400 to study the desert cockroach near Palm Springs, California. He was especially interested in the roach's diet.
- Foreshadowing future military madness, the Army spent millions in research and development in the late 1950s to create a jeep-mounted bazooka type of weapon that was capable of firing a nuclear-tipped shell. The Davy Crockett vehicle was introduced in 1961 and shipped off to NATO troops in Germany, for whom it was designed in the first place. But since the Davy Crockett had to be at least two miles from the enemy to fire a nuclear weapon, enthusiasm for its usefulness quickly waned, and the vehicles were stored in a warehouse.
- The Agriculture Department spent $63,600 to research bamboo, although none grew commercially in this country.
- Bryn Mawr College received $13,100 to study "octopus learning."
- NASA gave Michigan State University $40,000 to draw up a list of universities that it recommended NASA give research grants to. (Yes, it recommended itself.)
- Oklahoma State University received $29,000 to research the "social behavior of fish."

Of this last item, Representative Richard L. Roude-
bush (R., Indiana) protested: "I'm in favor of the fish being as social as they like, but it would appear outside the
realm of responsibility of the American taxpayer to finance a study of fish behavior toward one another"—a
sentiment still applicable today.

And finally, there's Project Mohole, or "the father of
the superconducting supercollider," circa 1965.

Project Mohole was a government-funded (through
the National Science Foundation) attempt to bore the
world's deepest hole ever, perhaps as much as four miles
down, starting on the floor of the Pacific Ocean. Its purpose was primarily to see what's there. "We think there
may be diamonds down there," said one geophysicist involved, "and some other pretty fancy minerals that the
United States doesn't have." In 1965 plans were well
under way to construct a huge drilling platform and actually to begin drilling in 1968.

Strangely, the whole idea of digging through the
earth's crust was hatched at a "wine breakfast" held by
members of the American Miscellaneous Society in 1957.
The group was an oddball collection of brilliant scientists who periodically got together to toss wild ideas off
one another. When the AMSOC decided to push seri-
ously for the Mohole project, it soon became affiliated
with the National Academy of Sciences and then acquired National Science Foundation money. When it was
revealed that Soviet scientists were considering such a
project, those around it began to present Mohole as a
race with the Communists as to who would be the first
to reach "inner space." The NSF immediately sank
$15,000 into the project to get it moving.

While scientists involved initially estimated that the
project could be accomplished with $5 million, they
soon revised costs up to $15 million and then to $35 million. By 1965 estimates had reached $50 million in capi-

tal expenditures and then another $10 million each year once the drilling started. Given the estimate that the drilling would take three years, the total package in 1965 stood at a whopping $80 million. In the meantime, millions were spent drilling test holes to prove concepts and test the limits of technologies. All the money was being funneled through the National Science Foundation, which soon began to question the number of contractors involved and whether they were working at cross-purposes. In June 1965 the Bureau of the Budget stepped in and ordered NSF to stop disbursing funds on Mohole until "the situation was clarified." Then congressional committees began to examine what some began to term "a hundred-million-dollar boondoggle." From that point on the project moved ahead slowly and fitfully, with construction of the drilling platform okayed and then more questions about spending until it all sort of ground to a halt, as these projects still do. Amid charges that President Johnson had backed the project to favor the principal contractor, Brown & Root, Inc. of Houston, in late July 1966 the House denied the requested $19.7 million for fiscal 1967, and the Senate concurred a week later.

The Judiciary

Think I'd leave out a whole branch of government? Well, in order to cover the range of bizarre judicial behavior and strange decisions at the federal level properly, an entire volume would be the necessary venue. However, the following is one of my favorites.

Why the Courts Are Really Backed Up

In 1993 U.S. District Judge Frederic N. Smalkin, in Baltimore, ordered attorney Timothy F. Umbreit to copy a portion of a lawbook in legible, longhand script. Umbreit had had the misfortune to argue before Smalkin that a case he was handling belonged in federal court. The judge ruled that the case really belonged in state court. When Umbreit persisted in his petition that the case be heard at the federal level, Smalkin said that he had become annoyed at "the gap in the counsel's knowledge of federal law." As punishment, he gave Umbreit thirty days to turn in his written assignment, along with certification attesting that the handwriting was indeed his own.

The Brave Few

Everyman Speaks Out, Gets Busted

Glen Kozubal, twenty-three, of Whitehall, Pennsylvania, sat quietly in the Senate visitors' gallery observing a long quorum call. Finally fed up with the lack of action, he leaned over the railing and asked, "You guys going to stand around here all afternoon?" After a Capitol police officer told him to remain quiet, Kozubal asked, "What, I can't talk to them?" That got him arrested and charged with a misdemeanor: "disruption of Congress."

Never Ask the Government to Prove Your Sanity

When Lloyd Miller of North Dakota died in 1984 at the age of seventy, he left $1 each to his four brothers and sisters and $1.3 million to the federal government. The family protested the will, and the case wound up in a North Dakota county court. The family's position was that Miller was insane. Witnesses described him as a man who lived in fear for his life, staying for eight years inside a house with all the windows boarded up. One witness related that Miller believed he was being spied on through the radio on his tractor. Attorneys for the federal government argued that it was simply a case of a man who didn't like his relatives. The jury ruled in the family's favor, and the will was voided.

Voices of Protest

In 1992 Matthew Lesko sent each of fourteen leading congressional figures a jar full of chicken guts with a note attached reading: "This is what you need to make some real decisions, to get this country moving again." Each jar was labeled with an expiration date of March 20, 1992, the deadline given by President George Bush as an ultimatum for Congress to deal with his tax program. However, the guts, which Lesko got from a slaughterhouse, spoiled en route, and the stench from the packages led at least one Senate office to contact the U.S. Capitol Police. Lesko said that the police then questioned him because they "wanted to know who I was, why I sent this. . . . I think they thought I was some kind of Jeffrey Dahmer. It's a good thing it wasn't post-marked Milwaukee." As for his motive, Lesko said, "I just got frustrated with how these leaders don't have the guts. It was for my own amusement."

- In protest of a Navy plan to build inexpensive hous-ing for sailors on parkland in Key West, Florida, Harry Powell, a former city commissioner, appeared at the site armed with dynamite and refused to sur-render until the General Accounting Office agreed to investigate the Navy effort. Just prior to taking over the site, Powell called the press to say: "This is Harry Powell, former city commissioner of Key

West. I have taken over Perry Court construction site. I have some explosives. I am trying to hold people at bay. . . . But there's a story that needs to be told about this project and how it was funded and what they're doing with the taxpayers' money. . . ." During the standoff he told the press, "If they're getting away with it here, they're getting away with it everywhere." After the GAO faxed police a statement saying that the Coast Guard, which was initially awarded the building funds, had not justified the housing need and that a "new review is in order," Powell surrendered, handing over two gallons of gasoline, three blasting caps, and a stick of dynamite.

• A United States district court ruled that the Virginia Department of Motor Vehicles had no right to cancel and recall the vanity license plates of Mark Steckbeck. The plates read GOVT SUX. State officials logged the first complaints about Steckbeck's tags, which had been issued by the state motor vehicle agency in the first place, after two state officials noted that he had paid his county tax bill of $1,188 in rolled coins. The state added Steckbeck's plates to a list it maintains of banned vanity plate messages, such as WORK SUX, VASUX, I95SUX, and THIGH. Judge Albert V. Bryan, Jr., ruled that Steckbeck's plates, as criticism of the government, were protected speech under the First Amendment. Said Steckbeck: "I'm happy to get the plates back. . . . My intention was, the government stinks."

Don't Blame Us

The Missouri Senate voted in 1994 to require all state auto emission inspection stations to post large signs reading "This inspection is mandated by the Environmental Protection Agency under powers granted to it by your United States Senators and Representatives in Washington, D.C."

I See a Trend Being Born Here

On the evening of April 15, 1994, with just hours to go before the midnight deadline, postal workers in Tulsa, Oklahoma, were collecting tax returns directly from motorists in a drive-through lane when a naked man drove up and handed over his return. The postal worker who collected from him quoted the man as saying, "Taxes this year have stripped me," and said that he was obviously looking to see if a live television crew had filmed him before driving off.

Nice Tries

Frustrated by a back-tax bill of $2.2 million, the Internal Revenue Service raided Robert C. MacElvain's Eufaula, Alabama, home in January 1993 and took four hundred items, including the family Bible and his wife's diamond ring, right off her finger. MacElvain's response was to file liens against the property of the IRS agent who had led the raid as well as the property of the locksmith who had helped the government gain entry to the home, the mover who had moved all the possessions, the appraiser who had set a price on each item for the government, and the man who had towed away his car as part of the seizure. He then placed a newspaper ad warning that the items to be sold at auction were "stolen goods." The IRS responded by indicting MacElvain on eight counts of "corruptly endeavoring to obstruct and impede the due administration of the Internal Revenue laws." A federal jury found him guilty on five counts, and he faces the possibility of three years in jail and a fine of $250,000.

- The IRS fined taxpayer Lawrence McCormick $500 for sending in his tax return with the following message under his signature: "Under protest." Brooklyn federal court judge Jack Weinstein ruled that the agency violated McCormick's First Amendment rights with the fine and ordered the agency to pay him back. "A taxpayer need not suffer in silent acquiescence to a perceived injustice," wrote Weinstein in his decision. McCormick said that he plans to continue writing his message on his tax return as well as attaching fifteen-page addenda detailing his opposition to the income tax system.
- After receiving seven days' notice to vacate his home so that the IRS could seize it in lieu of back taxes owed, Carl Jeffrey, forty-four, blew up the house and shot himself to death. "He was a gun enthusiast, so he knew all about black powder," said Phoenix police sergeant Tim Bryant. "He set three charges in there with black powder and ran lines to them so he could be in one place and ignite all three."

- The IRS paid Miami attorney Daniel N. Heller $500,000 to settle his claim that three agency employees violated his civil rights. According to a report in *The New York Times*, the trouble all started back in 1975, while Heller was general counsel of *The Miami News*. The paper reported on an IRS operation, dubbed Operation Leprechaun, in which it claimed the agency was illegally spying on the sexual and drinking escapades of prominent citizens. When the IRS believed the newspaper's information came from a source inside its own ranks, an agent asked Heller to name the source. The agent (whom the newspaper later identified as the leader of Operation Leprechaun) and Heller got into a "heated exchange of words" when Heller refused to name names. After he filed his tax return for 1976, the IRS investigated Heller for tax evasion, and one of the three agents assigned to the case was, again, the former head of Operation Leprechaun. An appeals court later determined that the agents had intimidated Heller's accountant into giving false testimony at his trial, leading to Heller's being convicted and jailed on a three-year sentence, of which he served four months before his conviction was overturned. "This five-hundred-thousand-dollar apology by the IRS is my total vindication," said Heller. "It proves I never cheated on my tax returns, never owed any money to the IRS, paid all my taxes on time, and was totally innocent of the trumped-up charges filed against me."

The Revolution Will Not Be Audited

In 1990 the IRS uncovered evidence of a group of tax protesters who were causing havoc by filing false 1099s that purported to show large payments having been made to a number of prominent government officials. The goal of the prank was to cause the agency's computers to detect the large discrepancies between what a targeted individual actually reported as income and the supposed income recorded from the false 1099 and cause audits to be initiated. One U.S. attorney, himself a target of false 1099s showing him as having been paid $32,334,010.58 in one tax year, said, "People who do this are trying not only to disrupt the IRS but our whole form of government." According to the *Wall Street Journal*, the IRS disclosed that between 1988 and 1990 it had detected about two thousand false 1099s from at least ninety-two sources and that it was planning criminal investigations. The first six people indicted in the investigations were facing five years in prison and $250,000 fines for each false 1099 filed. "For anyone who thinks this is just a prank, the indictments . . . ought to serve as a stern warning," said a former IRS commissioner.

Blow Those Whistles but You're on Your Own . . .

A 1993 General Accounting Office investigation into the Office of Special Counsel, the independent agency entrusted with protecting federal employees who "blow the whistle" in cases of waste and abuse, found that 88 percent of the whistle-blowers were the victims of reprisals for speaking out against the improprieties at their agencies, 47 percent saying that they were threatened with reprisals and 20 percent that the reprisals had come within twenty-four hours of their initial reports about waste and abuse. About 76 percent of the whistle-blowers said that they believed the OCS was acting in the interest of the agencies involved, not on the behalf of the whistle-blowers.

- A 1994 Nuclear Regulatory Commission report found that the federal government doesn't provide sufficient protection from reprisals for nuclear workers who blow the whistle on conditions at their plants. The NRC report noted that the current system encourages the plant workers to speak out about infractions to operating regulations but then "leaves them largely responsible for their own protection." The report recommended that Congress give the NRC the authority to issue $500,000 fines in cases where companies have retaliated against whistle-blowers.

Your $ Worth

Whoops!

Vice President Al Gore's National Performance Review, *Creating a Government That Works Better and Costs Less*, 168 pages in length, cost the government about $4 each to print. According to the Government Printing Office, the printing should have cost 90 cents each. The reason? The report "was produced on the best and most expensive Grade 1 coated paper (high gloss) in multiple ink colors, at Quality Level 2 (on a scale of 1 to 5) on a rush schedule over the Labor Day weekend." The total cost for two printings totaled $168,915. The normal cost would have been $54,091.

- The prices the Government Printing Office charges for its publications are also often suspect. For instance, its *Statistical Abstract of the United States*, a paperback nearly three inches in thickness, sells at GPO bookstores for $32. But according to the *National Journal*, in 1994 a private publisher, the Reference Press Inc., bought the negatives from the agency and issued the same volume under the title *The American Almanac*. With an improved glossy cover, it sold for only $14.95.

Top Desk

Between 1991 and the close of 1993 the Air Force spent
$511 million to train more than twelve hundred beginner
pilots only to end up assigning them to desk jobs because of a shortage of flight assignments. The General
Accounting Office estimated that the service might
spend as much as $195 million more training an addi-
tional five hundred pilots who would also be destined
for desk jobs. The cost is then compounded when these
"pilots" earn bonuses due all pilots as time goes by,
whether they fly planes or not. Also, once they do have
the opportunity to fly again, the Air Force will spend
anywhere from $64,500 to $74,400 per pilot in refresher
courses.

Get Me 250,000 George Listers!

An interim report by the State Department's inspector
general's office in 1993 targeted for termination George
Lister, a retired Foreign Service officer who has worked
as an unpaid consultant to the department's human
rights section since 1982. Among the charges leveled
against Lister were that he worked for free, worked
twice as many days per year as was authorized, and
went about making too many speeches in his free time.
Lister apparently was caught up by political infighting at
the department, according to *The Washington Post*,
which reported that political pressure from Lister's
friends in high places (he has long been a well-respected

expert in the field of human rights) saved his unpaid position.

Okay, I Know, We Make Everyone in America Sound Like Donald Duck for, Like, a Hundred Years

Since 1925 the U.S. Bureau of Mines has maintained a huge reserve of helium gas in Amarillo, Texas, in order to fuel the Army's fleet of dirigibles. Unfortunately the Army hasn't had a fleet of dirigibles for about the past four decades. As of 1993 the stockpile was valued at $1.6 billion, enough to last the United States a hundred years at current rates of use. Despite concerns in the early sixties that the helium would be needed for NASA space launches (which resulted in a crash program to pump more than thirty billion cubic feet of the gas into the huge underground reservoir), only a small fraction has ever been used. Now the operation employs 220 Bureau of Mines employees and has driven the agency $1.3 billion into debt. The question of shutting it all down is a complicated one. In the early 1960s the government, stuck on the idea that helium was of strategic importance, sought to create a helium industry by buying huge amounts and sending prices skyrocketing. However, now that some in Congress do want to close it down, the industry argues that to sell off the huge reserve would so flood the market with cheap helium that it would put them all out of business. When asked during her testimony before the House Budget Committee why the Clinton FY95 budget still did not eliminate the national helium program, then Office of Management and Budget

Deputy Director Alice Rivlin said, "I think we keep it for some mysterious political reason." Her questioner, Representative Christopher Cox (R., California), called the program "one of the dumbest programs [and] one of the easiest to get consensus on to cut."

No More for the Little Boy Who Lives Down the Lane

President Clinton in 1993 signed a bill to end forty years of subsidies paid by the federal government to wool and mohair producers. The subsidies began when the Pentagon put wool and mohair on the list of "strategic materials" because of their use in making uniforms and gloves for the armed services. The subsidies continued despite the fact that the two products were taken off the list in 1960. Estimated savings from the move, which phases out the subsidies over two years, are $514 million by 1998.

Hey! How Come Those Guys All Look like Fred Mertz?

When President Clinton criticized the Pentagon's stockpiles of products in military warehouses, things began to be moved out of storage pretty quickly. Several months after he fingered one storage area filled with 1.2 million bottles of nasal spray, the inventory was down to less than 2,000. The Pentagon also revealed that it had finally moved out much of its supply of pajamas and bathrobes dating back to the 1940s. The lucky recipients of those items were not revealed.

Federalism: The Practice of Accepting Only the Highest Bids for Any Project

An Associated Press survey of prices for items bought by the federal government to deal with the emergency flooding conditions in the Midwest in the summer of 1993 found that the government went out of its way to pay higher prices for sandbags and portable toilets than was necessary. The government rented portable toilets from a company in Kansas for $600 each per month while a closer outlet was renting them for $130. While many of the sandbags came from the Pentagon's unused stockpile from Desert Storm at only 5.3 cents apiece, 12.5 million bags were bought from commercial suppliers at rates of from 16 cents to 38 cents each.

You Can't Be Too Careful

According to a 1989 report by the State Department Watch, a private watchdog organization, the Department of State issued eighteen thousand travel expense checks without getting corroborating evidence for the expenses. One check for $9,000 was issued to "Ludwig van Beethoven," whose Social Security number was listed as "123-45-6789."

- When the United States attorney's office in Pikeville, Kentucky, sold its old computers, it forgot to erase confidential files from the machines' hard drives. The businessman who bought them discovered files going back for several years which contained lists of informants, sealed indictments, and the names of federally protected witnesses.

One More Job We All Should Have

In February 1993 it was revealed that the Resolution Trust Corporation had been paying thirteen hundred workers an average salary of $35 an hour to photocopy loan files at HomeFed Savings Association, a failed California thrift. The photocopying, being directed by the accounting firm of Price Waterhouse, was expected to total from $25 million to $30 million. According to the RTC's inspector general, the agency's contract with Price Waterhouse for the photocopying and "document management" was only two pages long and set no limits on the charges. The official said that labor costs for the photocopying were 67 cents per page for millions of pages. The inspector general also found Price Waterhouse billing the RTC with huge markups of its original costs. One billing manager was hired by the accounting firm for $1,505 a week from a temp agency. Price Waterhouse then billed the RTC $6,700 a week for the individual, at a markup of 345 percent. Price Waterhouse said that the "billings were reviewed prior to payment by a number of RTC personnel, including one of the senior vice presidents of the RTC. . . . There was no cost overrun on the HomeFed project."

Defense Money You Probably Never Knew You Spent

Back in 1980 the Department of Defense budgeted $370,000 to build an indoor kennel for twelve German shepherds at Fort Myers, Virginia. An Army veterinarian defended the cost in terms of how much money was spent to train the dogs in the first place. (Years earlier some taxpayers hit the roof when they learned that the Navy spent $45,968 to build a doghouse twenty-three feet by twenty-three feet to house two dogs at the Brunswick, Maine, Naval Air Base. Those two drug-sniffing dogs had a house costing $86 per square foot.)

Cults of Personality

In 1991 the Pentagon refurbished one hallway in its mammoth complex to honor former chairmen of the Joint Chiefs of Staff. The array of columns, special lighting, and framed photographs cost $519,000.

Yeah, but *Besides* That, Name Me One Reason Not to Fund It

In the mid 1980s the Pentagon's Sergeant York air defense system (formerly known as DIVAD—division air defense) had several embarrassing test performances. The weapons system (the cost of which would have totaled $5 billion if completed), which consisted of dual barrels and a sophisticated radar system mounted on a tank type of chassis, was supposed to track aircraft with its own radar system, aim, and hit its target. However, when it was rolled out and turned on in a demonstration before a reviewing stand full of senior officers and defense contractors, the gun swung away from its intended target and leveled its barrel on the reviewing stand, sending spectators running. At another test the gun, with its radar programmed to pick out the whirling blades of an oncoming helicopter, instead targeted the whirling blades of an exhaust fan in a nearby latrine. In further testing, special reflectors were attached to a target helicopter's rotor to help the DIVAD with its aim, but it still failed to find the target. Critics of the gun also charged that the system was too slow-moving to keep up with the tanks it was designed to protect, and it was found to be less effective against targets that didn't fly in a straight line. Finally, after a $54 million series of battle-field tests, the DIVAD was canceled.

Oh, Those Satellites!

A 1993 General Accounting Office report found that the Air Force spent $630 million for "communication satel-lites stored by contractors." However, upon further dig-ging, the auditors discovered that the satellites in question were "not on the Air Force's financial or prop-erty inventory or property management records." In short, there was no record of their whereabouts that the GAO could find.

- A misplaced part of a top secret Milstar military com-munications satellite, worth $360,000, was bought at a North Carolina auction by an auto mechanic for $75. The Pentagon later explained that the trucking company that was to transport the part (a super-sophisticated radio amplifier) from the defense con-tractor that had made it to an Air Force base lost the paperwork for the shipment, and the part was sent to the lost freight department, which turned it over to an auctioneer. The missing piece was detected, ac-cording to the *Wall Street Journal*, after the buyer lent it to a friend who was a ham radio operator. That man contacted the defense contractor, asking for operating instructions. The buyer noted that the Air Force investigators sent to retrieve the part "were a little bit huffy when they took it." He also related a conversation in which the investigators said that if the radio operator had gotten the part hooked up, it "would have knocked out every TV for two miles in every direction."

Justice with Style

In May 1994 columnist Jack Anderson reported that Representative John J. Duncan, Jr., (R., Tennessee) found that the proposed federal courthouse to be built at Fan Pier near downtown Boston would cost the taxpayers $218 million. The project made provisions for a six-story atrium, thirty-three private kitchens, thirty-seven law libraries, a marina, and a waterfront park, among other things. The budget for artwork alone for the new courthouse totaled $789,000. Duncan termed it the "Taj Mahal" of federal courthouses.

Pssstt! Want to Buy Some Zinc?

Since the 1950s the Pentagon has built up an inventory of strategic materials, the National Defense Stockpile, now valued at $6.3 billion. Designed to prevent the nation's being caught shorthanded in necessary raw materials in the event of a war, the stockpile includes diamonds, silver, aluminum, platinum, and zinc, among other items. The collection was amassed under a law requiring enough materials to wage a three-year worldwide conflict. Regulations which took effect in 1994 mandate that the stockpile now be sufficient to cover a "period of national emergency that would necessitate an expansion of the armed forces, together with a significant mobilization of the economy of the United States." While the emphasis has shifted from acquiring and maintaining the stockpile to selling off as much of it as possible, the new problem is how to do that without further damaging a market already flooded by strategic materials being sold by the former Soviet Union, which is selling off its supply for the same reason: raising cash to help solve budgetary problems.

My New Project's Titled "Art in My Wallet"

Three artists in California, recipients of a $5,000 grant from the National Endowment for the Arts, designed a "public art project" called "Art Rebate." It consisted of their taking their federal grant dollars in the form of $10 bills and distributing them to immigrant workers. They handed out $4,500, while $500 went for such expenses as printing handbills announcing what the artwork was all about. According to one artist, the "main purpose of this project is to insist we expand the parameters of the immigration debate." Another said, "We are rebating taxpayers' dollars to taxpayers. Undocumented workers have [Social Security] taxes withheld from their wages, and they also pay sales taxes. . . ."

Davy Jones, Call Your Office

A Pentagon inspector general's report released in 1989 revealed that the Navy was sinking its surplus ships without first stripping them of valuable equipment. The report stated, "We feel confident that public property valued in excess of $17 million was destroyed." Among the items that could have been retrieved and sold were new mattresses (still in their plastic packaging), bandsaws, milling machines, motors, and lathes, as well as all types of furniture, gold and silver (in the communications equipment), brass, copper, ovens, radio equipment, cryptologic equipment, surgical equipment, and pumps. Investigators inspecting retired ships that were destined to be sunk noted the presence on board of numerous spare parts that were still being bought by the Navy.

Give a Boy a How to Fish Politely Handbook, and He'll Fish Politely His Whole Life ...

A General Accounting Office report said that in 1991 the Fish and Wildlife Service was so concerned about the misconduct of participants at bass fishing tournaments that the agency spent $250,000 to purchase copies of the thirty-two-page booklet *How to Conduct (and Conduct Yourself in) a Bass Tournament.* The booklet, published by Anglers for Clean Water Inc. of Montgomery, Alabama, did have a price on it of $1.95. However, the publisher was distributing the booklet free of charge to anyone who requested it.

Cost Effectiveness 101

The Customs Service released six helium-filled balloons fitted with surveillance equipment to patrol for drug smuggling along the Mexican border in 1991. The balloons cost $90 million to construct and $30 million to operate for thirty months. During that time agents seized only three thousand pounds of marijuana and nine weapons. That works out to about $40,000 spent by the program for each pound of marijuana seized. Senator Dennis DeConcini (D., Arizona) defended the project by suggesting that the small amounts of drugs seized proved that the balloons were a deterrent to smuggling.

So What Else Is New?

In 1988 Congress passed the Computering Matching and Privacy Protection Act, a law designed to regulate, among other things, how agencies gather and use data in computer matching programs—the searching of two or more data bases to compare the names, addresses, Social Security numbers, and other data on individuals listed to see if they are somehow defrauding the federal government. For instance, such matching is a way to determine whether someone is really eligible for welfare benefits or if a federal worker is delinquent on a student loan. However, a 1994 General Accounting Office investigation of the procedure found that 41 percent of the federal agencies using the technique made no estimate of the cost or benefits of such a procedure. The GAO also determined that in 59 percent of the cases where a cost/benefit analysis was done, "not all reasonable costs and benefits were considered, inadequate analyses were provided to support savings claims and no effort was made after the match to validate estimates." Thus the government doesn't really know whether a procedure designed to curb waste and fraud is really doing the job.

Cool! A Glow-in-the-Dark BarcaLounger!

Federal investigators have discovered that the Department of Energy's contractors are unable to account for tens of millions of dollars' worth of equipment. Senator John Glenn (D., Ohio) said that the department "has lost or could not account for . . . computers, forklifts, furniture, welders, X-ray machines, and even a semitrailer." One contractor stored furniture and other equipment alongside radioactive material at the Fernald nuclear weapons facility in Ohio. All of it then had to be buried at a Nevada nuclear test site.

Next Up, Judge Crater

Responding to a request from Representative Steven
Schiff (R., New Mexico), the General Accounting Office
has opened an official investigation to determine if the
U.S. Air Force has suppressed information concerning
UFOs, specifically the supposed crash of a flying saucer
in Roswell, New Mexico, in 1947. (The incident, a favorite among UFO fans, reportedly involved the Air Force's
at first issuing a news release on July 2, 1947, reporting
the crash of a saucer only to change the story within
hours to say that a weather balloon had crashed.) Schiff
asked the Department of Defense for a briefing on the
matter but was told that all relevant documents had
been turned over to the National Archives. The Archives,
of course, said that they had no Roswell documents.
Said Schiff: "Generally, I'm a skeptic on UFOs and alien
beings, but there are indications from the runaround
that I got that whatever it was, it wasn't a balloon. Apparently it's another government cover-up."

Sticker Shock

Late in 1993 the GAO informed Congress that the total
cost of the Central Arizona Project, a large water aqueduct designed to pump water uphill from the Colorado
River to farms and the cities of Phoenix and Tucson,
may cost $1.1 billion more than expected, for a total of
$4.7 billion when completed. The extra charges include
$157 million in possible defaults on federal loans to

farmers in the area, $585 million that the government may have to assume in settling Indian water rights claims, and $400 million in a contract dispute between the U.S. Bureau of Reclamation and local officials. After all that, the aqueduct is being operated at only one third its capacity because cotton farmers in the region are buying far less water than was expected.

So, You Mean They Feel the Same Impact of Federal Dollars That Our Own People Do?

A report by staff members of the Senate Foreign Relations Committee concerning the state of the $3 billion U.S. aid program to the former Soviet states concluded that the program has management problems and that the money may not be directly affecting the average citizens of those countries. "It does not appear that the average citizen of Moscow, Almaty, or Bishkek—let alone the vast majority of citizens who live thousands of miles away from these urban areas—is aware of or affected by international assistance or the reforms that it is supposed to foster," the report said. Government engineers in one city that received new energy equipment from the United States "admitted that the average citizen does not feel the effects of the program since there is no change in energy output to the consumer." In another region a public opinion poll found 79 percent supporting privatization of government industries but also showed that 50 percent of the respondents didn't know the meaning of "privatization."

Flash! Jesse Helms Has Good Idea!

Foreign diplomats in Washington, D.C., owe the city about $6 million in unpaid parking tickets. Fed up with the fact that such fines are regularly ignored by the foreign embassies, Senator Jesse Helms (R., North Carolina) introduced an amendment to the 1994 foreign aid bill that would require that all parking fines plus a 10 percent penalty be deducted from any U.S. foreign aid money destined for a country that has not paid its tickets. According to *USA Today*, Russia owes $4 million in tickets, Egypt owes $77,830, Nigeria owes $146,030, Zimbabwe owes $65,640, and South Korea owes $73,480.

One Good Deal

The Bureau of the Public Debt consists of a commissioner, currently Richard L. Gregg, and a professional staff of 1,850. These people, working on an annual budget of $165 million, manage our nation's debt on a day-to-day basis. It stands at about $4.5 trillion at this writing. Besides managing the debt through huge redemptions and sales of government securities several times each week, the office provides Senator Jesse Helms (R., North Carolina) with the exact daily national debt figure (fifteen digits long—down to the penny) each day the Senate is in session so that he can remind his colleagues each day from the Senate floor.

Homer Simpson, Call Your Office

In the 1980s five workers at the Department of Energy's Rocky Flats nuclear facility in Golden, Colorado, were fired for "engaging in a water fight and other horseplay during the night shift." Following the water fight, three men bound a fourth with plastic tape like a mummy and were about to lift him up using a crane when a supervisor walked in on them. Rocky Flats was the manufacturing center for plutonium triggers used in nuclear weapons.

- In December 1993 the Department of Energy announced that Westinghouse, the manager of its Hanford nuclear reservation, would receive no bonus (or "earned award fee") for the six-month period ending in September of that year. It was the first time since the program started in 1976 that a contractor was denied a bonus by the agency. The award would have totaled at least $2 million. The decision not to issue the bonus followed a period during which one worker died from burns suffered when a steam pipe ruptured and another created a situation in which radiation was dispersed due to his decision to use a rock tied to a rope to try to unclog a pipe leading from a waste tank full of hazardous material. In the latter incident the worker reportedly acted out of frustration with established safety regulations.

I Want My Extra Sense Organ Now!

The government regularly spends money to sponsor gatherings of scientists who either are asked to tackle specific problems or are encouraged to propose their own theories and inventions. Every year since 1960 the Jasons, a top secret group of about forty scientists, gather to work on specific government projects for such agencies as the Pentagon and the CIA. The scientists, the tops in their fields, are paid at least $500 a day (as of the late 1980s) for sessions lasting about six weeks. The government also sponsors gatherings of futurists— scientists who are paid to gather and exchange their visions of "what if." A report in 1987 about one such meeting sponsored by the Air Force revealed the results of the government-paid "brainstorming session": a proposal to implant computer chips in the brains of jet pilots to give them "an extra sense organ," a suggestion that human body parts could be grown as replacements, the idea of running computers by thought wave, and the design of biological "diseases" that could be specifically developed to enter and "eat" the insides of an enemy's computer system. (If the price is right, I shall reveal my theory that we all should have our own "transporters" like those on *Star Trek*. It would be too cool.)

Scamming the Federal Government 101: Advanced Students Only

In 1991 a scandal arose when it was revealed that major universities were charging the federal government for outlandish practices and writing them all off as "research costs." Among other things the taxpayers got stiffed for were: chauffeuring the president of Dartmouth College and his wife ($20,490), MIT's contribution to the Museum of Fine Arts ($4,655), Cornell University's purchase of Steuben glass wine goblets ($1,000), and Stanford University's purchase of a cedar-lined closet ($3,000), the refurbishing of a grand piano ($2,500), the cost of monthly flower arrangements at the home of a university president ($2,000), and the depreciation charged on a yacht ($184,286).

But Seriously, Folks . . .

Senator John Glenn (D., Ohio) charged that Westinghouse, as a contractor to the Department of Energy, transferred almost $1 million of taxpayers' money to the Westinghouse Electric Corporation, an affiliate in Washington, D.C., for the purpose of lobbying. "Basically, the GAO discovered that the government was paying to have itself lobbied by Westinghouse," Glenn said. The GAO said that some of the federal money was used for "legislative monitoring and liaison activities" and that the Washington office was supposed to represent Westinghouse's interests in meetings with the Energy Department, the Office of Management and Budget, and Congress. Westinghouse said that there was no lobbying performed, just "legislative monitoring and reporting." According to the GAO, when Westinghouse questioned the allowability of its own expenses, it was advised by lawyers that it was acceptable. That legal bill was also paid by the government—$3,613.

Paying $ to Stop Spending $

According to an item in *The Progressive*, Congress authorized $1.7 billion in 1994 to "allow for the orderly termination of the B-2 [bomber] program." $790.5 million of that sum was allotted for "research and development"! The balance of the allotment goes toward purchasing five more B-2s. And although there is a moratorium on nuclear testing, the authorization bill also provided $217.4 million "to support the readiness of the Nevada Test Site to resume testing, if necessary, at a future date."

The "Death Star" of Government-Funded Science Projects

The Department of Energy's Superconducting Supercollider project was a sinkhole for federal funds from day one. The ambitious plan called for the construction of the most powerful atom smasher ever built in a huge circular underground tunnel fifty-four miles long. After the department awarded the winning site location to Waxahachie, Texas, it was discovered that the spot was infested with fire ants. Then the department spent $1.4 million to send the environmental impact statement on the project to sixteen thousand citizens who had simply expressed interest in it. The law required that the agency provide each with a summary of the statement. Instead it mailed the entire twenty-five-pound, eighty-eight-hundred-page statement to each person. With cost estimates growing every year, debate raged in Congress and in the scientific community on the wisdom of putting so many tax research dollars into one place. In 1993 the total for the project was estimated to be $11 billion. Finally, in the fall of 1993, Congress voted to kill the project, and the President signed the bill. At its death the SSC project was one fifth complete. Left beneath Waxahachie are a fourteen-mile-long tunnel and a complex of laboratory buildings. The $640 million originally intended to fund the program for one year was instead allotted to the cost of shutting it down. Said Senator J. Bennett Johnston (D., Louisiana): "Ten years into this project, three presidents, $2 billion, 10,000 employees, all devoting their lives to this and all of a sudden the country loses its nerve." According to a plan worked out to compensate the dislocated workers at SSC, each received sixty days severance pay and a $15,000 "dislocation allowance." More than two thousand were eligible for the deal. Among the structures left behind at the site is a central office complex that cost $30 million to build and is the size of nine football fields. The first person to make a pitch for alternative uses for some of the complex was the president of a Texas company that owns one mushroom farm and wants to try to grow mushrooms in the SSC underground tunnel. Negotiators for the federal government and the State of Texas have proposed a plan to divide the program's assets that would allow the State to use the buildings to create a cancer research center, a supercomputing headquarters, and a magnet development lab.

Sources

Associated Press
CongressDaily
Congressional Quarterly
Greenwire
Harper's
Insight
The National Journal
The New York Post
The New York Times
The New York Times
  Magazine
Newsweek
Parade
People

The Philadelphia Inquirer
The Progressive
Reuters
Saga
States News
The Syracuse New Times
Texas Monthly
Time
USA Today
U.S. News & World Report
The Wall Street Journal
The Washington Monthly
The Washington Post
The Washington Times

Plume   **Dutton**

COMIC RELIEF

☐ **IF CATS COULD TALK by P.C. Vey.** Here are 90 hilarious cartoons concentrating on our furry little feline friends and just what they might be thinking and saying about people. It's more fun than a ball of yarn.   (266424—$6.00)

☐ **EXCUSES, EXCUSES by Leigh W. Rutledge.** A witty, enormously entertaining compendium of Rationalizations, Alibis, Denials, Extenuating Circumstances, and Outright Lies.   (269210—$6.00)

☐ **IT SEEMED LIKE A GOOD IDEA AT THE TIME *A Book of Brilliant Ideas We Wish We'd Never Had.* by Leigh W. Rutledge.** Filled with hundreds of outrageous oversights, idiotic innovations, and preposterous proposals, this uproarious assemblage of ill-advised notions proves once more that to err this big can only be human.   (271894—$5.95)

☐ **LATIN FOR PIGS *An Illustrated History From Oedipork Rex to Hog & Das.* by Lisa Angowski and Virginia R. Blackert. Illustrated by Harry Trumbore.** This irresistibly humorous compendium of the distinguished individuals and great moments of history and culture illuminates the porcine past as never before. You'll find profiles of such influential oinkers as Pigmalion, Albert Einswine, Pablo Pigcasso, Robin Hog, Sadham Hogsain, as well as classic works of literature like *Oinkle Tom's Cabin*.   (938206—$10.95)

Prices slightly higher in Canada.

Visa and Mastercard holders can order Plume, Meridian, and Dutton books by calling
1-800-253-6476.
They are also available at your local bookstore. Allow 4-6 weeks for delivery.
This offer is subject to change without notice.

Ⓟ **Plume**

STRANGER THAN FICTION

(0452)

☐ **BEYOND NEWS OF THE WEIRD by Chuck Shepherd, John J. Kohut and Roland Sweet.** News Junkies of the world, rejoice! Gathered here in one hilarious volume are more than 500 of the weirdest, craziest, most outlandish true stories ever to find their way into our nation's newspapers.

(267161—$8.00)

☐ **MORE NEWS OF THE WEIRD by Chuck Shepherd, John J. Kohut and Roland Sweet.** Just when you thought it was safe to read the Sunday papers comes this volume with over 500 of the most bizarre, the most shocking, the most unbalanced stories—you won't believe your eyes.   (265452—$8.00)

☐ **NEWS OF THE WEIRD by Chuck Shepherd, John J. Kohut and Roland Sweet.** Just when you thought you'd already heard it all, here comes this hilarious volume with over 500 strange-but-true stories that proves once and for all that facts are far weirder than fiction.   (263115—$9.00)

Prices slightly higher in Canada.

Buy them at your local bookstore or use this convenient coupon for ordering.

PENGUIN USA
P.O. Box 999, Dept. #17109
Bergenfield, New Jersey 07621

Please send me the books I have checked above.
I am enclosing $_____ (please add $2.00 to cover postage and handling). Send check or money order (no cash or C.O.D.'s) or charge by Mastercard or VISA (with a $15.00 minimum). Prices and numbers are subject to change without notice.

Card # _____ Exp. Date _____
Signature _____
Name _____
Address _____
City _____ State _____ Zip Code _____

For faster service when ordering by credit card call **1-800-253-6476**

Allow a minimum of 4-6 weeks for delivery. This offer is subject to change without notice

℗ **Plume**

A HUMOROUS LOOK AT LIFE

☐ **IT'S ABOUT TIME by Michael D. Shook and Robert L. Shook.** Hundreds of fascinating facts about how we spend it, fill it, buy it and defy it.   (268524—$9.00)

☐ **JUST SAY "NO CAR KEYS"** *and Other Survival Tactics for Parents of Teen-agers* **by Shelley Goldbloom.** Believe it or not, you can survive the pangs of growing pains. This humorous, irreverent guide can help see you through the trials of adolescence (theirs, not yours!) with style, grace, a pound of salt, and a generous helping of revenge.   (269377—$8.00)

☐ **NEWS FROM THE FRINGE** *True Stories of Weird People and Weirder Times* **Compiled by John J. Kohut and Roland Sweet.** In this hilarious volume . . . are gathered more than 500 of the weirdest, craziest, most outlandish stories to grace the pages of the world's newspapers. . . . A phantasmagoria of lethal library fines, fetishes on parade, love that's a many splintered thing, least compe-tent criminals, neighbors from hell, anal retentive suicides, and much more.
                                                              (270952—$8.00)

☐ **A ZILLION AND ONE THINGS THAT MAKE MOMS CRAZY by Shelley Goldbloom.** If the trials of the terrible two's (and three's and ten's) are getting you down, let this delightful book of domestic misadventures take you away from the indelible ink artwork your toddler just left on your new wallpaper.
                                                              (269822—$6.00)

☐ **BOSSES FROM HELL** *True Tales from the Trenches.* **by Matthew Sartwell.** In this hilarious yet horrifying collection of unhinged employers there are tales so incredible they have to be true. Bosses from hell. Everyone's has one.
                                                              (270480—$7.95)

Prices are slightly higher in Canada.

Buy them at your local bookstore or use this convenient coupon for ordering.

PENGUIN USA
P.O. Box 999, Dept. #17109
Bergenfield, New Jersey 07621

Please send me the books I have checked above.
I am enclosing $_____ (please add $2.00 to cover postage and handling).
Send check or money order (no cash or C.O.D.'s) or charge by Mastercard or VISA (with a $15.00 minimum). Prices and numbers are subject to change without notice.

Card # _____ Exp. Date _____
Signature _____
Name _____
Address _____
City _____ State _____ Zip Code _____

For faster service when ordering by credit card call **1-800-253-6476**

Allow a minimum of 4-6 weeks for delivery. This offer is subject to change without notice

Ⓟ **Plume**

WILD & WITTY

☐ **COUNTDOWN TO THE MILLENIUM Compiled by John J. Kohut and Roland Sweet.** "Disturbing yet darkly humorous . . . *Countdown to the Millenium* is a handbook of hysteria that invites you to panic now and avoid the rush."—*New York Times News Service*   (269156—$8.00)

☐ **ONLY IN CALIFORNIA by Janet Hearne.** Brimming with bizarre facts, irreverent trivia, anecdotes , quotes, statistics, slogans, license plates, epitaphs, and more. This unique collection serves as a lone letter to the idiosyncracies and oddities that indeed make California the country's "most altered state."
                                                                                (270022—$8.00)

☐ **MERDA!** *The REAL Italian You Were Never Taught in School.* **by Roland Delicio.** A humorous, uncensored guide to the off-color colloquialisms that are so essential to a true understanding of everyday Italian. Shocking idioms . . . hard-core curses . . . pithy epithets for every nasty occasion . . . detailed descriptions of insulting hand gestures . . . and much more.   (270391—$9.00)

☐ **SCHEISSE!** *The REAL German You Were Never Taught in School.* **by Gertrude Besserwisser.** Illustrated by David Levine. If you think you have a fairly good command of German, think again. This hilariously illustrated cornucopia of creative expletives, guaranteed to vex, taunt, aggravate, and provoke as only overwrought low German can, will help you master the fine art of German verbal abuse—with triumphant one-upmanship.   (272211—$7.95)

Prices slightly higher in Canada.

Visa and Mastercard holders can order Plume, Meridian, and Dutton books by calling
1-800-253-6476.
They are also available at your local bookstore. Allow 4-6 weeks for delivery.
This offer is subject to change without notice.